SAINTS
OF THE
TWENTIETH
CENTURY

By the same author:

Live and Pray (with Sister Geraldine, Dss CSA)
Pray with . . . (with Sister Geraldine, Dss CSA)
Private Prayers
More Saints of the Twentieth Century
Youth Prayer
Pocket Calendar of Saints & People to Remember
(Revision of) *Year Book of Saints*
Into Your Hands
(Revision of) *Everyman's Book of Saints*
From the Fathers to the Churches (Editor)
Day to Day (Editor)

SAINTS
OF THE
TWENTIETH
CENTURY

Revised Edition

by
BROTHER KENNETH, CGA

MOWBRAY
LONDON & OXFORD

© Community of the Glorious Ascension, 1976, 1987

ISBN 0–264–67110–4

First published 1976 in hardback by A. R. Mowbray & Co.
Ltd, and in paperback by Lutterworth Press

This Revised Edition published 1987 by
A. R. Mowbray & Co Ltd, Saint Thomas House,
Becket Street, Oxford, OX1 1SJ

Typeset by Spire Print Services Ltd, Salisbury
Printed in Great Britain by Biddles Ltd., Guildford

British Library Cataloguing in Publication Data

Kenneth, *Brother*, CGA
 Saints of the twentieth century.—Rev. ed.
 1. Christian biography
 I. Title
 209'.2'2   BR1700.2

 ISBN 0-264-67110-4

Acknowledgements

The author and publishers would like to thank the following for permission to print certain passages: Catholic Truth Society; Creation House; Epworth Press; Gill & MacMillan Ltd; Hodder & Stoughton Ltd; Longman Group Ltd; Overseas Missionary Fellowship; SCM Press; SPCK; St Vladimir's Theological Quarterly; Routledge & Kegan Paul Ltd; Word Books.

Extracts from the New English Bible c 1961, 1970 by permission of the Oxford and Cambridge University Presses. In addition the author would like to acknowledge with gratitude the help, and in some cases permission to print original material, of the Librarians and Archivists of: The American Baptist, Foreign Mission and Historical Societies; Australian Board of Mission; Church Missionary Society; Council for World Mission; Fellowship of St Alban & St Sergius; Methodist, Archives and Missionary Society; Sacra Congregatio Pro Causis Sanctorum; St Paul's Cathedral, London; United Society for the Propagation of the Gospel. He would also like to thank the staffs of Birmingham City; the Catholic Central, Gloucester City and Stroud County Libraries; Dr Broomhall of the Overseas Missionary Fellowship; the Community of the Resurrection of Our Lord; Father Bus and Father Wiltgen of the Society of the Divine Word; Sister Gerarde Salemink of the Missionary Sisters, Servants of the Holy Spirit; 'The Orthodox Word'; Mr Vladimir Anderson; Father Yves Dubois; Mrs Helena M. Lambert; St George Orthodox Information Service and Mr N. Mabin; the Bishop of Lincoln; the Bishop of St John's, SA; Mr John Stirland; Miss Pauline Webb; Miss Edith Wiseman; Mr Herman

Hemingway; Mr Leslie Hartley; Mrs Violet Redlich and the Revd Leslie Wright.

Finally the author records his incalculable debt to Mrs Connie Tyrell of Northampton who in gracious, loving and of necessity, patient friendship, deciphered his handwriting, acted as secretary and typed the original manuscript.

Contents

viii *Contents*

Introduction

Recognizing Saints

If no Church makes a Saint, that being God's prerogative, occasionally his work is recognized and a Church
accords to certain of its members a kind of hero-
worship signified by such titles as *Saint* or *Blessed* or
Venerable. Three Christian Communions are prepared
to name their saints: the Roman Catholic, the
Orthodox and the Anglican. The first two who
together comprise a good two-thirds of Christendom,
actually use the title Saint; Anglicans are generally less
specific and simply add the name of a new Saint to
their Calendars, and are tentatively followed in this by
the Church of South India.

At the head of each biography is given a suggested
date for the commemoration of the saint or the
appointed feast day in the Calendar, which is not
necessarily the date of death.

Martyrs were the first Saints to be honoured. *Martyr*
is originally a Greek word and means 'witness', but it
came to be particularly employed of those who could
have saved their lives if they had been prepared to
deny Christ. Gradually the honour paid to the martyrs
was also given to those who, though witnessing a
good confession, managed to die in their beds.

Official recognition of sancity began as a strictly
local affair. The fame of certain saints, often encouraged by stories of miracles occurring at their tombs,
spread and thus Christian heroes would soon be
commemorated liturgically in areas far removed from
the scenes of their earthly labours or the places where
they died. Many parish churches in Cornwall or Wales
bearing dedications to obscure local saints are present
day evidence of those saints whose fame did not travel

very widely. Canonisation by popular acclaim still occurs; witness the prayers offered today at the tomb of Oscar Romero in San Salvador.

In Western Christendom it was not long before the authority to declare a new saint was claimed exclusively by Rome, and by the end of the sixteenth century a standard procedure for canonisation had been developed by the Papacy. It is still in essence the system adopted by the Roman Catholic Church today, and as might be expected, it is extremely thorough. To some Christians, however, it seems pointless that those who acknowledged Pope John XXIII as the earthly head of the Church should insist that a prolonged, complicated, not to say scandalously expensive procedure must be followed before Rome officially proclaims what has all along been obvious—namely that in Angelo Roncalli God has made yet another Saint.

Orthodox Christians have never surrendered the principle that new saints are acclaimed by Christians at large. Way back in the fourteenth century a Patriarch Philotheos was defending a canonisation that some thought had happened rather too quickly after the Saint's death, on the grounds that 'the sight of things which are manifest cannot be called into question'. John Maximovitch, the very holy Synodical Russian Orthodox Bishop of San Francisco who died some twenty years ago is already being revered as a saint especially in the United States and Canada. Canonisation is not the regular term which the Orthodox use to describe the naming of a Saint. Rather they talk of his 'Glorification', thus emphasising the end not only of the particular Christian, but of all God's people who are destined to be like Christ.

Thirteen of the Saints or groups of Saints here have been declared such by their respective Churches. In addition if the naming of a church building after a particular Christian be an overt act of canonisation, Dietrich Bonhoeffer must be added to that number. Martyrs make up the second group. At least two, Abdul Karim and Manche Masemula died expressly because they were Christians. The remainder were killed as they fulfilled their Christian duty, and a number including Abdul and Manche are recorded in the Book of Modern Anglican Martyrs kept in St Paul's Cathedral in London. All told there are thirteen Saints or groups of Saints who were martyrs. A further nineteen remain, right across the ecclesiastical spectrum, including missionaries, like Hudson Taylor and Mary Slessor, great preachers like William Sangster or 'Woodbine Willie', founders of Communities like Charles de Foucauld and Florence Allshorn and at least one very ordinary woman but extraordinary Christian, Winnie Letts. In each case they appear primarily because their fellow Christians saw Jesus plainly reflected in their lives, and because within their respective ecclesial settings, their names are still revered, and their examples held up before the faithful.

Sociological Sanctity

Calendars of every Christian Church are depressingly clerical. That is the only excuse which can be offered for the fact that so many of the Saints in this book are clergymen, monks and nuns or some kind of official representative of their churches. According to three sociological investigations[1] into Roman Catholic canonisations, 50% of all their Saints held high office within that Church. Up to 1953 of a total of 2494 Saints, over 75% came from the upper echelons of society and only 5% could possibly be called working-class. There is no doubt that similar figures would be obtained for other Churches while the Saints of the pre-revolutionary Russian Orthodox Church are almost exclusively Religious or ordained and from a military background.

Obviously any officially recognized Saint is a reflection of what his church at any one time considers to be sanctity. The pattern changes from century to century and from church to church, and is bound to be affected by sociological and economic factors. A large number of Twentieth Century Saints were involved, for instance, in questions of political and social reform. However the ghastly popular assumption that sanctity can only be expected from among those who are actively and officially involved in the ecclesiastical hierarchy is evidence that for far too long the Church has been satisfied with what amounts to a double standard of Christian commitment.

Homesick for God

'The Saint is God's greatest work,'[2] a Twentieth Century one wrote that and presumably he ought to know. Of course Saints never do know. One of the marks of true sanctity is deep humility. It is never simply the result of moral struggles. Saints become Saints not because 'God loves them and attends to them more than he does to us: but because they love and attend to him more than we do'. Goodness is a gift from God, but he does not force-feed us.

The Oecumenical Patriarch, first among equals of all the Orthodox bishops, when asked in 1931 for a definition of a saint, referred the questioner to St Paul in his letter to the Galatians. 'I have been crucified with Christ: the life I now live is not my life, but the life which Christ lives in me' (Gal. 2.20). If we can say of any saint that he is like Christ, then we have also declared our conviction that in certain respects Jesus Christ is like the saint.

Heroic Sanctity cuts right across the denominational boundaries. This should not surprise us for the same Holy Spirit is responsible. Saints use different language according to their particular Christian or cultural heritage but over and over again they say the same things or behave in similar ways. Whatever their background the Saints are evidence of what God can accomplish and has accomplished in men and women who respond to him. The saints can quicken in us a desire for holiness and convince us that it is no pipe-dream. They should make us 'homesick for God'.

At the end of each biography there is a short prayer. Often it is an adaptation of something the Saint wrote or said. The prayers are brief and will stand repetition—perhaps as arrow prayers.

William Porcher DuBose, a delightful Confederate clergyman—in his day a theologian of international repute and now commemorated in the Calendar of the Episcopal Church of the United States—wrote, 'It is infinite initial blessing, a present Gospel to us, that God does not wait for us to be good; that he takes us to himself from the minute of the birth in us of the will to be good, and by treating us as though we were, makes us good.'[3] Reading or hearing about a saint is sometimes the means whereby that 'will to be good' is born both in us and our children.

Candlemas, 1987   Kenneth CGA

Notes

1. *Altruistic Love*, P. A. Sorokin, Boston, USA, 1950 Roman Catholic Sainthood & Social Status, K. & C. H. George in *'Journal of Religion'*,

Vol 35, Chicago, 1955 *Sociologie et Canonisations*, P. Delooz, La Haye, 1969
2. *The Pure in Heart*, W. E. Sangster, London, 1954
3. *An Apostle of Reality*, T. D. B. Bratton, London, 1936

Gladys May Aylward 1902–1970

(1 JANUARY)

Glady's was sitting on the edge of a narrow bed in a not very glamorous bedroom at the top of a house where she had just been employed as a maid. She was thirty years old and desperately sure that God wanted her to go out to China as a Missionary, yet the famous China Inland Mission having allowed her a term's trial in their training college had refused her because they said she was just not bright enough and would never be able to learn Chinese. Gladys knew she had been hopeless at school. She'd tried hard but invariably came at the bottom of the class. Nonetheless she was sure God wanted her in China; she had taken this new job in order to earn enough for her fare. Beside her on the bed were her bible, a devotional book, and about threepence in coppers, all the money she possessed in the world. The train fare to China then was nearly forty-eight pounds. It would take her a long time to save that amount. She closed her eyes and prayed, 'Oh God! Here's me, here's my bible, here's my money, use us God, use us.' She prayed intently but suddenly heard her name being called. Her new mistress wanted her. She hurried downstairs to discover that it was the practice of the lady of the house to pay the fares of her maids when she engaged them; she wanted to know how much it had cost Gladys and promptly paid her the three shillings. Gladys went straight upstairs and added the money to her store. She saw it as coming straight from God towards the journey to China.

On Saturday 15 October 1932 she did eventually set off to join an old missionary at her station in Yangcheng, a town in Shawhi Province about five miles from the left bank of the Chin Ho, a tributary of the Yellow River and some 360 miles as the crow flies south west of Peking. Gladys had never actually met Jeannie Lawrence, but had heard how Jeannie, who was single-handed and in her seventies, had returned to China to die.

On her journey from the port of Tientsin Gladys had exchanged her European clothes for Chinese ones and at Yangcheng she changed her name too and was called Ai Weh Teh. Jeannie Lawrence had had the idea of turning the courtyard of their home into an inn so that some of the muleteers who travelled across the mountains would turn in there, and thus provide the two women with opportunities for telling them about our Lord. To Gladys was given the job of persuading the travellers to stop off at the inn, and their cook assured her that the right approach was to call out in Chinese 'No fleas! No bugs! Good Good. Come! Come!'

When Mrs Lawrence died the income that supported the mission ceased, but Gladys was quite unexpectedly appointed by the civil authorities as Inspector of Feet for Yangcheng and the surrounding villages. Such an official was necessary to ensure obedience to the laws enacted against the practice of binding up girls' feet, thus crushing the toes, all in the interest of a social custom that insisted that refined young ladies must have tiny feet. In the major cities it had been largely abolished but in the country districts it was still a common practice. At government expense, and accompanied by two soldiers Gladys was able to tour the whole district preaching Jesus Christ. It was then that she developed her remarkable gift for storytelling which was to hold her audiences throughout her life. The people of Yangcheng accepted her completely as one of themselves, but she wanted to be one of them in everything so she destroyed her British passport and became a natural-ised Chinese citizen.

After Japan invaded China she was frequently in Tsingcheng. The mission station there was flooded with refugees from either the Communist forces of Chu Teh and Mao Tse Tung or the Japanese. Among the refugees were over one hundred children and the Christians were terrified of their being captured by either the Reds or the Japs. One spring morning in 1940 Gladys and one other adult set off with the children on a journey of over 200 miles across rugged mountainous country to Sian, south of the Yellow River. The story of that incredible journey was the basis of a book by Alan Burgess called *The Small Woman* and later of a film *The Inn of the Sixth Happiness*. The latter caused Gladys much pain for it included several scenes which had no basis in fact at all.

Gladys and her charges had food for only two days; thereafter they relied on what she could beg and the pity of the villagers they met. At the Yellow River they waited for two days almost in despair for a boat and were eventually ferried across by the army. They were denied entrace to Sian which was full of refugees and at length found shelter sixty miles further on at Fufeng. At the end of that journey, her task completed and the children safe, Gladys became so ill that her friends feared for her life. She did recover physically, but for a long while she was mentally disturbed, not knowing who or where she was, and this condition was to afflict her from time to time for the remainder of her life.

Peace was shortlived in China after the defeat of Japan. The Communist army was pressing forward and it would not be long before they took over the whole of the mainland. Gladys's sympathies were with the Nationalists, so when she wanted to return to China after two separate visits to England, where she was technically a foreigner with a Chinese passport, she settled in Taiwan, the large island off the coast of China and the only remaining strong-hold of the Nationalists, Free China as they called themselves. It wasn't long before Gladys was immersed in work with children again. She was very happy in Taipei at the Northern tip of Taiwan going out preaching every day and as busy as could be.

One night someone broke into her house. They hadn't taken anything. She herself has described what happened. 'They'd left something behind. They'd left a baby. There it was lying in my room, and I looked at it and I said "Oh no, Lord, no! Definitely no. I don't want any more babies"', but she finished by telling God 'All right Lord. If you want me to take in babies.' She loved the work nonetheless but it was to be a cause of great sorrow to her when the man whom she trusted to run what turned into a big orphanage, embezzled large sums of money. She had to give evidence at his trial. In a letter to a friend also in trouble about this time she wrote,

> 'I know exactly what you are going through because I am going through the same thing . . . It seems as though everything I do is wrong and only my faith in a loving and living God keeps me going, because I get one bang after another.'

Another of those bangs was the film 'Inn of the Sixth Happiness,' but she goes on 'I believe that God has called you and me and it is not to walk as other people have walked in a nice rosy way, but just along the way he walked to Calvary . . . One day we will know and understand why.'

It was her faith that most inspired others. A schoolboy heard her speak. When asked what impressed him he answered, 'It was the way she talked about God—as though she knew him'. She did, and on 1 January 1970 she entered more completely into His presence.

PRAYER: *Lord I'm here. What I have is yours. Use us.*

* * * * *

Ivan Illich Sergiev (John of Kronshtadt) 1829–1909

(2 JANUARY; *old calendar 20 December*)

Once, when he was a boy, Ivan Sergiev saw himself in a dream as a priest in a strange Cathedral. He was ordained in December 1855 and when, with his wife, he went to take up his first appointment at St Andrew's Cathedral, Kronshtadt, he was deeply moved to discover it was the very Church he had seen in his dream. In those days Kronshtadt was the island to which all the petty criminals and down-and-outs from St Petersburg were deported. Beside them were large numbers of unskilled workmen employed in the docks. They lived on the outskirts of the town in shacks, and many were beggars and drunkards. Here Ivan began his lifelong ministry to the outcasts of society.

Daily he went to their wretched dwellings to talk to them and comfort them in their miseries. He nursed the sick and helped the needy. He gave away all he had, so that many a time he would come home minus some of his clothes, or even without his shoes. He had dedicated himself to trying to restore the self-respect that his poor people had long since lost, for he saw them all as made in God's likeness. He soon discovered that he had been given the gift of healing. By his prayers and the laying on of his hands the most severe illnesses, often those which the doctors had pronounced past hope, were cured. Such events could not be concealed and soon hundreds of people from all over Russia began to converge on Kronshtadt. So many would write to him that the Post Office set aside a special department for his mail and soon he was receiving large sums of money to use for relief of the poor.

With this money Father Ivan would feed up to one thousand destitute persons daily. He established in Kronshtadt a work shelter with a school, a church, workshops, and an orphanage. In his native village he founded a nunnery, and built a large stone church, while in St Petersburg he built a nunnery in Karpovka, where he was to be buried.

He used to rise at 3 o'clock in the morning and prepare himself for celebrating the liturgy. At about 4 o'clock he went to the Cathedral for Matins. Here crowds of pilgrims would be waiting to ask for his blessing and many beggars wanting his help. St Andrew's Cathedral, which could hold up to 5,000 people, was always filled to capacity, so that the Eucharist often did not end before noon. After the service Ivan would leave for St Petersburg to visit the sick, and would rarely be home before midnight. His fame as a healer was his heaviest burden for wherever he went he attracted crowds, striving even to touch him.

In 1893 he published a remarkable book *My life in Christ*. It was really his spiritual autobiography and it still has a great impact on its readers. Politically Ivan, while anxious to be of service to all in need, did not want to see the destruction of the Russia he knew and he was out of sympathy with the liberal ideas that were becoming increasingly popular there.

He died on 2 January 1909. Thousands came to his funeral and the Requiem was more like the triumphant Orthodox Easter Celebrations. Joy was in every heart.

PRAYER: *Lord let me feel I need you: that way I know you'll be near me.*

Ivan Sergiev was canonised by the Synodical Russian Orthodox Church as St John of Kronshtadt in 1970.

*   *   *   *   *

Jim Elliott
and Companion Martyrs   1956
(8 JANUARY)

The five young men all came from the United States. Jim had wanted to be a missionary since High School days in Illinois. At Wheaton College he deliberately chose to study Greek and records his joy when he first read the story of the Passion of Our Lord in St John's Gospel. 'The simplicity and pathos made me almost weep, something which has never occurred in my English reading. Surely it is a wonderful story of love.'

By 1950 he was convinced that God was calling him to preach the Gospel in Ecuador, and in particular to a little known and savage tribe, the Aucas. The Aucas hated the white man and with some reason. The need for rubber within industrial nations brought many rubber-hunters to the Amazon in the middle of the last century. The majority of these men were completely unscrupulous. They bribed the Aucas with worthless trinkets and when they had gained the Indians' trust raided their villages, plundered their goods, and carried off the able-bodied young men to work as slaves on the plantations. The remainder of the inhabitants would be murdered. The Aucas understandably wanted no dealings with the treacherous white man.

In 1952 with his wife Betty, and his friend Pete Fleming from Seattle, Jim sailed for Ecuador. In the capital, Quito, they spent six months learning Spanish and from there journeyed seventy miles north east to a Mission Station at Shandia, among another Indian tribe called the Quichuar, a gentle people quite unlike the head-hunting Jivaras to the south or the much feared Aucas who lived further inland. A year later another college friend of Jim's, Ed McCully with his wife and young son joined them at Shandia. Ed had come from Milwaukee and at one time had considered becoming a lawyer.

Shandia's contact with Quito and other missionary bases was maintained by a small Piper plane of the Missionary Aviation Fellowship. Its pilot was Nate Spring, a Philadelphia man. He had joined the fellowship when demobbed from the services after World War II and in 1948 he and his wife had been sent to Ecuador. Nate had often flown over Auca territory and when he heard from Jim Elliott and his friends of their plan to preach the gospel to the Aucas he asked to be included in the team. He found its fifth member Roger Youderian, who with his wife Barbara and their two children, lived and worked at another mission station at Macuma in Jivaros' territory.

Roger too had served in the war, eventually becoming a paratrooper, and was decorated in 1944. It was in Berlin, in 1945, that he began to wonder if God wanted him to be a missionary, and he and his family arrived in Ecuador in January 1953. Two years later they joined the other four at an outpost established in Arajuno about twenty miles south east of Shandia.

To begin with they had to find some of the Auca and then try to make contact with them, by dropping gifts. The first one, a small aluminium bottle, some bright buttons and rock salt was dropped on 6 October 1955. To this they had no response and saw nobody but slowly, gift by gift, they seemed to gain the people's confidence and on one occasion were actually given something in exchange.

Next they needed a suitable spot to land, not too far from the Auca settlement which they had nicknamed 'Terminal City'. A beach in the Curarey river was found; that they called 'Palm Beach'. On 3 January 1956 it took five flights between Arajuno and 'Palm Beach' to bring in all their equipment, which included enough material for them to make a tree shelter. Nate also flew over 'Terminal City' to invite the Aucas over a public address system to visit them at 'Palm Beach'. The five men were very disappointed when three days had passed and they had had no visitors. On the fourth day, a Friday, a man and a woman did venture into the open. Jim and the others were overjoyed. Surely when they returned safely others would follow them. Nobody came on the Saturday, but next day Nate flew over the settlement and reported that he had seen a band of Aucas making for their camp. 'Looks like they'll be here for the early afternoon service', he joked over the radio to the wives waiting at base. 'Pray for us, this is the day! Will contact you next at four-thirty.'

When Nate's wife switched on the radio that afternoon at 4.30 sharp not a crackle broke the anxious silence. Not one of the five was alive to answer. All had been speared to death. In his diary Jim Elliott once wrote 'O Jesus, Master and Centre and end of all, how long before that Glory is Thine, which has so long waited Thee? Now there is no thought of Thee among men; then there shall be thought for nothing else. Now other men are praised; then none shall care for any other's merits. Hasten, Hasten, Glory of Heaven, take Thy Crown, subdue Thy Kingdom, enthral Thy creatures.'

Two or three years after her husband's death, Betty Elliott was back in Ecuador, living among the Aucas.

PRAYER: *Praise and honour, glory and might, to Him who sits on the throne and to Jesus his son for ever and ever.*

* * * * *

Mary Mitchell Slessor   1848–1915

(13 JANUARY)

On the walls of her home in West Africa there hung a photograph of a Scots family. The husband had sent it to Mary Slessor for he always said he owed his soul to her. They had met when he was a young man in Dundee and Mary worked in a Mission set up in his rough district of the town. One night as she was going to the mission hall he and his gang surrounded her. Swinging from his hand was a heavy leaden weight tied to a piece of cord. Mary was forced to stop. The boy swung the weight threateningly round her head.

Mary stood her ground. The weight shaved her brow; still she looked straight at her tormentor. The weight crashed to the ground. 'She's game boys', exclaimed the boy. That night the entire gang went to the mission.

Mary was a Scotswoman, having been born in a suburb of Aberdeen on 2 December 1848, but when she was eleven years old her family had moved to Dundee. Her home was a difficult one, for her father was a drunkard and she had had to help with the family income as soon as she was old enough to work. She had little formal schooling but became a voracious reader so that by the age of twenty eight and after a short period of training in Edinburgh she was sent out as a teacher to a Mission Station in Southern Nigeria.

The infamous Slave Trade by which Europeans were able to impress labourers for their sugar plantations in the West Indies drew most of its slaves from West Africa. It is one of the unhealthiest spots in the world, especially for Europeans, and the lot of the native Africans was not much better. By religion they were largely Animists convinced that any catastrophe was the work of malign spirits who could only be placated with blood. Politically they were ruled by their chiefs who could inflict the most savage punishments for any real or imaginary offence detected by the witch doctors. If a chief's son should die for instance, the witch doctor might declare that his demise was the work of evil spirits conjured by the chief of a neighbouring village. In expiation a raid would be carried out and innocent victims dragged from the offending village to be cruelly executed at the boy's funeral. To such warlike and savage people did Mary set sail on 5 August 1876.

For her first two tours of duty she lived and worked in established Mission Stations between the River

Cross and the River Calabar about 100 miles west from the modern border between Nigeria and Cameroun, but in 1888 she wrote 'I am going to a new tribe up country, a fierce cruel people, and everyone tells me that they will kill me. But I don't fear any hurt; only to combat their savage customs will require courage and firmness on my part'. She had plenty of both and countless are the wars she stopped, the twins she saved, the abandoned children she rescued, the floggings she prevented. Almost single handed she set up a station at Ekengo among the Okoyong tribe and lived with them for fourteen years.

When she went there it was an area regarded with fear by the coastal Africans and unexplored by Europeans, for they knew it to be given over to ritual murders, ordeals by poison or boiling oil, and perpetual war between villages. Mary was responsible for stamping out many of these evil customs for she came thoroughly to understand the tribesmen's language and their ways of thought. She gained an extraordinary ascendency over the men, especially the chiefs in much the same way as she had controlled the gang of rowdy lads in Dundee and when Britain took over the rule of the area it was Mary whom the Governor appointed as judge for the Okoyong.

Prayer was the mainstay of her life. It was there that she gained strength to smile and persevere under the most appalling circumstances. 'If I am seldom in a triumphant or ecstatic mood' she once wrote, 'Christ is here and the Holy Spirit. I am always satisfied and happy in His love.' 'Prayer is the greatest power God has put into our hands for service—praying is harder work than doing, at least I find it so. There lies the way to advance the Kingdom.' 'We are not really apart,' she once wrote to a friend in Scotland, 'for you can trust God direct by prayer, and so can I.'

During 1908 Mary suffered continual bad health and was unable to do much outdoor work. Among other ailments she was troubled for a time with boils which covered her entire body. On one of her many journeys from Use to Ipke she met with a slight accident when a pellet of mud stuck in her eye and she was blind for a fortnight, but she was soon back at work as if nothing had happened. Like St Paul she was full of concern for the young churches and was continually aware of all those in Calabar who had still to hear the good news of Jesus Christ. Her final illness began soon after Christmas 1914, and she died after much suffering on 13 January 1915.

PRAYER: *Lord make me strong and resolute, not fearful or dismayed for you are with me wherever I go (Joshua 1.9).*

* * * * *

Yona Kanamuzeyi   1918–1964

(23 JANUARY)

Yona began courting the girl of his choice by pouring into the young lady's ear all the unsavoury details of his past life. Few young men can have begun a love affair like that, but Yona had told God he would accept it as a sign from Heaven if Mary still agreed to marry him after she had heard the worst. She did accept him, and they were married on 13 October 1945 at Gahini about forty miles North East of Kigali and twenty miles from their country's border with Tanzania.

Yona was a teacher and evangelist of the Rwanda

Mission and a year after their marriage he and Mary were posted to pioneer work in Gikomero, not far from the main road at Shyira that leads into southern Uganda. They had to build their own hut, to say nothing of a church room but Mary and Yona were convinced that it was what God wanted and were happy. A year later when Mary went into the local hospital for the birth of their first child, complications set in and although their daughter was safely delivered, Mary nearly died. Her sickness made it obvious to the church's leaders that life at Gikomero was too hard for her and so Yona was appointed Pastor, though not ordained, to the church at Shyogwe, a little further to the South. He remained there until he entered his final two years of training for the ministry in 1958 and confidently expected to be sent back there as its minister, but in 1960 the Bishop asked him to go to the growing refugee settlement at Nyamata in the east of the country.

When Yona was a lad Rwanda, as a result of World War One had passed from being a German colony to Belgian control. While he was at Shyogwe African political parties had begun the movement towards independence, but it was never simply a matter of African self-government. Over three quarters of the population in Rwanda belong to the Bahutu tribe while the remainder are Batutsi. The latter group had become a ruling minority over the centuries and had retained much of their authority, prestige and privileges during colonial rule, so that the head of the government appointed by Belgium was the Batutsi king, Rudahigwa.

In August 1959 he died rather mysteriously and in the subsequent upheaval thousands of the Batutsi from the North West fled from their homes and the marauding Bahutu. Political ideas throughout the country quickly polarised along the tribal divisions and round two parties, Monarchist and Republican. By 1962 Rwanda had become an independent republic, and Batutsi refugee shanty towns like that at Nyamata were developing. Resentment among the Batutsi was rife and frequently directed not against the Bahuru, their fellow countrymen who had dispossessed them of their homes, goods and lands, but against the Europeans whom they believed to be ultimately responsible for their distress.

When in 1960 Yona first arrived at Nyamata for a preliminary six weeks, he found much going on. An efficient and very considerate Belgian administrator headed a team charged with the task of developing the refugee settlements. Roads were being built, and plots marked out for each family. Meanwhile the people were crowded in temporary sheds of corrugated iron, subdivided into little rooms eight feet square for each family. Coming from a comparatively rich area these Batutsi now had to accustom themselves to poverty and squalor while epidemics of typhoid and dysentry broke out as numbers increased. It was without doubt an uninviting spot but at the end of his six weeks, Yona went to fetch his wife and children and with other Christian leaders he worked happily among the people of Nyamata. Most of the refugees were Christians, both Catholics and Protestants and it was not long before Yona was regarded as the latter group's leader. Various international bodies such as Christian Aid, and Oxfam used to channel funds to support the refugees through the local churches and soon Yona was being asked for advice from all quarters.

From the time of the first troubles in 1959 until 1963, while the rest of Rwanda was in great turmoil, the refugees in Nyamata lived in peace, and Yona's influence was in a large measure responsible for this state of affairs. The church too, grew in numbers, but despite the outward calm trouble was brewing. A comparatively small number of the Batutsi had never resigned themselves to the republic. Ruthless guerilla bands known as Inyenzi, 'Cockroaches', began to operate and after each outrage more and more of the Bahutu looked upon every Batutsi as an enemy. Rumours of an army of Inyenzi trained in the neighbouring monarchy, Burundi, circulated and on 19 December 1963 these rumours were transformed into facts. When they arrived at Nyamata, many of the refugees hid from the invaders; others no doubt joined them willingly enough; yet others were forced to do so on the threat of instant death. The Rwandan army quickly routed the rebels but then exacted vengeance on many of the refugees, innocent and guilty alike. Within an hour of the defeat of the invaders, Nyamata was surrounded by troops firing on all sides. A reign of terror was instituted and Christians came in for a fair measure of abuse. At his morning services Yona regularly led his people to pray for deliverance, 'from blindness of heart, envy, hatred, and malice, and all uncharitableness'.

In January a friend came to him and told him he was going to be killed. 'There are no charges against you' his friend reported, 'but you stand for the word of God . . . and you love everyone indiscriminately.' Threats were thereupon regularly directed at Yona, and his wife and friends begged him to leave for a while. He refused. Andrew, Headmaster of Nyamata Primary School finishes the story: 'On Thursday 23 January 1964 at seven o'clock in the evening, a jeep with six soldiers arrived in front of the pastor's house and he was called outside. He went with a stout heart, trusting God. Two of the soldiers came to my house and told me I was also wanted. When I went outside I found my friend Yona already there. They told us to climb into the jeep. We went off with a third prisoner towards the town, Kigali, where we thought we were being taken. When Yona saw we were going towards this town, he said to me: "Let us surrender our lives into God's hands". He did not say this because of any evil he had done, but because for many days he had seen the soldiers taking people away like this and they never returned.

'We continued on our way, crossing the river, and a little way on the farther side we saw about eight more soldiers. They ordered us out of the jeep and told us to surrender anything we had. The third prisoner had a small suitcase which he put on the ground and I put my watch on this case.

'Yona then asked permission to write in his diary, and he wrote: "We are going to heaven . . ." and then he added, as carefully as he could in the time, an account of the church francs left in his house. He placed this diary with the key of his cupboard on the case, as well as a few francs from his pocket, and asked the soldiers to see that his wife was given these things.

'One soldier then said, "You had better pray to your God". So we all stood up and Yona prayed thus: "Lord God, You know that we have not sinned against the Government, and now I pray You to look upon our innocent blood and help these men who know not what they are doing. In the name of Jesus Christ our Lord, Amen."

'Then we were ordered to sit down and they brought rope and tied our arms behind our backs. One soldier was told to lead Yona away, but before he went we sang a hymn. When he had finished singing they took him away and, as he went, he asked me, "Do you believe?" and I said "Yes, I believe, because we read that whoever believes will be saved." He went singing. The soldiers took him back to the bridge over the river. There they shot him and threw his body into the water. I was left sitting with the third prisoner and the other soldier. They were all amazed; they had never seen anyone go singing to his death or walking as he did, like a man just taking a stroll.

'The soldiers then called me to them and I went. They ordered me to sit again and asked if anyone had an axe or a knife and I knew that perhaps they were going to cut me up as they had done many others. They asked me my name, and then they returned my watch to me. I asked them to keep it and to send it to my wife, but they ordered me to put it on. They then put me in the jeep again and, leaving the third prisoner on the road with some of the soldiers, we returned to the camp. They called at the house of the Roman Catholic headmaster, and then told me to go home, adding that if I said a word to anyone about the killing of our pastor, I too would be killed.

'God in His mercy later sent a man to lead me through the bush so that I might flee to another country where I have found refuge.

'But the death of this man of God amazed those soldiers who saw him die because he truly died as a man of God, praying for his enemies and for himself. He did not fear death because for him, as for all other saved people, death is the door to heaven.

'As for me, who have been saved from this bodily death, it has taught me again that God wants to save me from the second death which is the final judgment, to save me through faith in Jesus Christ who died for us, and I before him repent of my sins. And you who read this testimony—God is asking you to be strong in him and to profess him before men till the day when perhaps you too may be called to stand before those who would kill you, as Pastor Yona did.

'I Andrew, whom God has saved from death, write these words, and they are true.'

PRAYER: *From blindness of heart, envy, hatred and malice and all uncharitableness Good Lord, deliver me.*

Yona Kanamuzeyi's name appears in the Anglican Book of Modern Martyrs in St Paul's Cathedral, London.

*   *   *   *   *

Manche Masemula   1913–1928

(4 FEBRUARY)

Animism is one of the earliest religions. Animists believe that all of the natural world, trees and rivers, rocks and mountains, animals, birds and reptiles, sun, moon and stars, and all natural phenomena, wind and rain, thunder, lightning, sunrise and sunset, light and darkness, life, birth, growth and death are inhabited or controlled by spirits. The Ancient Britons were Animists and there are traces of Animism in the Old Testament in such things as Abraham's tree at Mamre (Gen 18.1–9) or Jacob's stone pillow (Gen 28.10–19). Animism is still a real religious force in some parts of the world and was stronger over half a century ago when Manche Masemula was born in a little village just outside Pretoria, the capital of what is now the Republic of South Africa.

Manche belonged to a part of the country that had taken its name, Sekekuniland, from a warrior who had led a rebellion first against the Boers and then the British in the nineteenth century. In Manche's village the people were all Animists. They lived in fear of the Spirits, a fear carefully nurtured by the Witch-doctors. Whenever the crops failed, or a child was ill, or a cow died, the witch-doctor would be called in to decide which spirit was annoyed, and why, and what had to be done about it. Droughts often exacted a fearful toll of human sacrifice.

Manche, on her way home from the fields where she had been working, heard a heart rending scream which she quickly recognised as the cry of her young cousin. It wasn't long before she had climbed a hill to see if she could help him only to be confronted by a terrible sight. A group of the villagers with the witch-doctor were dragging the boy off to sacrifice him to the spirits of the weather and thus bring to an end, they hoped, the drought that had afflicted their village for weeks.

There was nothing a girl of fourteen could do but run as far from that horrible sight as she could. Manche ran away, not knowing or caring where, towards a neighbouring village and only stopped when she heard someone call her name. It was the village Christian priest. Fear was in her face but she dared not tell him what she had seen. When she burst out that she had been frightened by an evil spirit, she was promptly invited to the priest's hut that night to hear about 'a great good spirit, the most powerful in all the world, who can take away our fear'.

Manche accepted the invitation and very soon was a regular visitor to the Christian village joining in its worship and becoming a member of its Guide Company. Soon she was longing for Baptism even though she knew it would provoke much hostility from her own family and village.

One day Manche became ill. She was provided with some medicine but she did not improve. Her family were furious that she had gone to the Mission doctor for help and scoffed at her because the Christian witch-doctor's medicine had not cured her. They insisted that she could not lie on her bed all day, but must get up to work in the fields as usual. That night the village headman and the witch-doctor with a crowd of villagers came for Manche and took her to a hut not far from the spot where her cousin had been killed. She was shut in all night, and next morning brought before the assembled village. She refused to give up her belief in the Christian God and there and then she was beaten to death by her own parents. Her body was wrapped in a blanket for burial. Twice they tried to dig a grave but each time their tools struck stone. This alarmed her murderers. Perhaps they had underestimated the power of the Christian's God? They sent for Manche's priest but he was away. An old man from his village was brave enough to come and Manche was buried in a spot that he chose. At fifteen Manche became a martyr, baptised in her own blood.

PRAYER: *I have made a vow to the Lord and I cannot go back (Judges 11.35).*

Manche Masemula is commemorated in the Calendar of the Anglican Church of the Province of South Africa.

Cecile Isherwood 1863–1906
Peter Masiza c 1850–1907

(20 FEBRUARY)

A dying mother in hospital at Port Elizabeth in what is now the Republic of South Africa clung to the hand of a nun visiting her. The wretched mother had sold her baby to a Malay family, but now realising what she had done, begged Sister Cecile to rescue the child. The Sister went immediately to obtain a magistrate's order, and, accompanied by a policeman, set off for the Malay house. A large group of Malays huddled about the door, an ominous sign. Suddenly Cecile, spotting the child, ducked under the crowd, seized it, tucked it up the capacious sleeves of her habit and fled. The mob followed her to the railway station, but she escaped with the baby unharmed.

Cecile had come to South Africa from England in 1883, as the result of a sermon by the Anglican Bishop of Grahamstown who had appealed for workers in his diocese. Cecile responded and before she sailed for South Africa, the bishop, at her request, made her deaconess.

She had not been in Grahamstown long when the Bishop confided in her his hopes. He wanted a community of nuns in his diocese and he wanted her to start it. She was then twenty-one and had had no idea of becoming a nun when she left England, but she thought about it and on 25 April 1884 she became the first novice of the Community of the Resurrection of Our Lord. She was quickly joined by other women and by the end of 1886 the sisters were living and working in both Grahamstown and Port Elizabeth.

In Grahamstown they ran an industrial school to

provide a home for destitute girls. St Peter's school followed and soon after that a free school for poor children. 'For three weeks' wrote Cecile, 'our first and only pupil (at the poor school) a child of seven, taught me missionary patience.'

At the start Cecile and her sisters were very poor. Food was so short that if a visitor stayed for dinner one of the sisters would have to go without. They only had one pair of strong boots and one lamp. One day an African priest called. He wanted to see the ladies 'with their heads tied up'. As he left he pressed some money into Cecile's hand. When she asked what it was for he replied 'For your Sisters'. 'But we are doing nothing for your people' Cecile protested. 'No, but you will.' Cecile treasured that gift. It was a direct answer to their prayers for there was no money in the convent that day. Later she was to write 'The attitude about natives and native work makes my blood boil. Certainly the church can never do enough to make up for the great wrong our white race has brought to them'.

In 1896 her community took over the training school and elementary schools for native Africans in Keiskama-Hock. Four years earlier Cecile and her sisters placed St Peter's school, Grahamstown, under government inspection. She wanted all her community's educational work to be brought into line with that provided by the State and to accept the State's standards and certificates of efficiency. In its turn the authorities pressed upon her the need for more and more teachers of both Dutch and English extraction in all grades of schools. So it was that with financial help from the government, a teacher training college was begun for women students in Grahamstown.

In her short life Cecile showed the characteristic graces of the saint—deep sacrificial love for her Lord and courageous, self-effacing compassion for her fellow-men, meeting poverty, opposition and apparently insuperable obstacles with infectious joy.

She died in England at the age of forty-four. Before an impending operation, in what she knew might be her last message to her sisters, she instructed them to 'peg away at strengthening simple personal religion in prayers, bible reading and Holy Communion'. This was no pious platitude. For many years she had been up very early every morning in order to spend an hour in prayer before the corporate morning prayers of her Community. In any difficulty her favourite expression was always, 'We shall have to go to work on our knees'.

She survived the operation for a few days and died on 20 February 1906. Anglicans of South Africa commemorate her in their calendar along with other modern Christians. Among them is a South African priest, Peter Masiza, who died a year after Cecile. He was born near Winterberg and brought up as a Lutheran Christian. While training to be a teacher at Zonnebloem he became an Anglican, and in 1877 was the first African to be ordained priest in the Church of the Province. He worked first at St Mark's Mission in the Transkei, and was then sent to Tsomo where he converted large numbers of the people and established a well-organised parish. He was an eloquent preacher, gratefully listened to by black and white alike. He was a model of a faithful parish priest, patient in his encouragement, stern to rebuke, and filled with pastoral love for all his people of every age and race. Could it have been Peter who pressed that money into Cecile's hand?

PRAYER: *Lord I can't do much, but I can do a little, and you can do a great deal with me* (Hudson Taylor).

Both Mother Cecile and Peter Masiza are authorised commemorations in the Anglican Church of the Province of South Africa.

* * * * *

Edward King   1829–1910

(8 MARCH)

Edward King did not go to school. His father was the Vicar of a village in North Kent, but Edward was born and baptised in London. He was never a very strong boy and for that reason he received his lessons from his father's curate. When the curate moved Edward went with him to continue his education. His eldest sister, Ann, was an invalid for twelve years and Edward spent long hours at home with her, trying to amuse her and help her forget the pain. He was always ready to fetch her a book, pour out her medicine or do any of the many jobs that invalids cannot manage for themselves.

When he had finished his education Edward went on a pilgrimage to the Holy Land, stooping down in order to go through the little doorway which leads to the church of the Nativity in Bethlehem, following the Sorrowful Way in Jerusalem, praying at the spot where our Lord's body was placed on Good Friday evening and in the garden where Mary Magdelene saw Him alive on the first Easter Day. Edward never forgot that pilgrimage and throughout his life frequently referred to it in sermons and letters.

In 1855 he was ordained and became curate of the little village of Wheatley, five miles outside Oxford. There his continual interest in the crops and in the gardens of the villagers, together with his knowledge of horses (he was an excellent horseman) helped him to gain the confidence of his parishioners. During his curacy an epidemic of typhus broke out. Edward insisted on visiting the worst cases himself, because, he said, the Vicar of the parish had a family.

One dark foggy night, he was summoned to the bedside of a sick man, who lived in a lonely farmhouse at the other end of the parish. It was a long walk and Edward was quite alone so he hurried as much as he could, but when he arrived he was astonished to discover that the call had been a hoax. Many years later, when he had become Bishop of Lincoln, he was visiting Lincoln gaol and one of the prisoners said to him, 'You have never known how near you once were to death. Do you remember that night, it must be thirty years ago now, when you were called out to visit a farmer who wasn't sick?' The Bishop nodded and the man continued, 'I sent that message. I had not had a square meal for days, I was hungry and desperate. I intended to knock you down, kill you maybe, and rob you'.

'Why didn't you?'

'As you approached I saw there was someone beside you and I did nothing.'

Edward remained at Wheatley for three years but he was always remembered by his parishioners. Once a poor man, who admitted that he had not been to church for a very long time and didn't intend going again, said there was only one thing that would persuade him to go. 'If I could only hear a chap named King preach', he said, 'then I'd go. I heard him at a village called Wheatley and I shall never forget him. I remember that there sermon though it's years ago since I heard it.'

In 1885 in St Paul's Cathedral, London, King was

consecrated Bishop of Lincoln. During his episcopate he got to know really well every parish in the diocese. He liked taking Confirmations in country churches best, or preaching at Harvest Festivals there. After one of his visits to a country church a boy who had been confirmed asked his mother 'Do they always send an angel from heaven to confirm you?'

Once, when staying at a vicarage, he was told about a farm hand who, when asked how he prepared himself the night before to receive Holy Communion, said 'I's cleaned my boots and put 'em under the bed'. The Vicar had been rather upset by this reply but King, with a merry twinkle in his eye, said 'Don't you think the angels would rejoice to see them there? They would say, "That means Communion tomorrow".'

Capital punishment for murder was the law in England then. The chaplain of Lincoln prison one day called on his Bishop. A young fisherman from Grimsby had been sentenced to death and was now in the condemned cell. The chaplain was young and inexperienced so the Bishop went to prison himself to see the man. That a Bishop should go to see a murderer in gaol was unheard of, but such was King's love for the condemned man, and so earnestly did he speak of God's forgiveness through Jesus Christ, that the prisoner repented, was confirmed, and the Bishop celebrated the Holy Communion for him in the condemned cell just before he was executed.

Edward King remained at Lincoln for twenty-five years. When he was eighty he became very ill and knew that he would not recover. Just before his death he dictated his last letter to the people of his diocese; it included this summary of King's ministry. 'My great wish has been to lead you to become Christ-like Christians.' Six days later he died. A friend, in a letter after the funeral at Lincoln Cathedral wrote, 'Today, we have buried our Saint'.

PRAYER: *Almighty God, you gave such grace to your servant Edward King that whoever he met he drew nearer to you; Fill us with sympathy as tender and deep, that we also may win others to know the love which passes knowledge; through Jesus Christ, your Son, our Lord. Amen.*

In 1935 on the fiftieth anniversary of Edward King's enthronement as Bishop of Lincoln he was publicly commemorated at a special service in Lincoln Cathedral at which the Archbishop of Canterbury was present. It was the first such commemoration since the Reformation in the Church of England, apart from the addition of King Charles the Martyr to the calendar. In the ASB 1980 Edward King's name appears in the calendar.

*   *   *   *   *

Geoffrey Anketell Studdert Kennedy   1883–1929

(8 MARCH)

'I know what you're thinking, here comes a bloody parson.' That's how Geoffrey Studdert Kennedy began at the smoking concert held at St Pol in Northern France for the men of the 4th Army School and their guests in 1917. Throughout his life he startled and often annoyed some of his listeners by such language, but for thousands of men and women of his day he was the only man who could make God and Jesus Christ real, expressing the most profound truths in language that could be understood and appreciated by the simple and uneducated.

He was born and brought up in Leeds, where his father was Vicar of St Mary's, Quarry Hill. The family came from Ireland which explains why Geoffrey completed his education at Trinity College, Dublin. While he was undecided about his future career he became a schoolmaster at West Kirby in the Wirral but teaching soon helped him to make up his mind to be ordained. It was at Ripon Hall, a Theological College in Oxford, that he first developed his own style of preaching and it quickly became clear to the authorities that here was an orator of considerable power.

He was made deacon in 1908 and appointed curate to the parish of Rugby. And a most unusual curate he was for he became very unhappy if he did not have to preach at least twice on a Sunday. His views were not always the most orthodox; all his life he knew what it was to doubt. He wrote not long before his death 'Everyman, whether Christian or not, must sooner or later stand in the last ditch face to face with the final doubt. I know that last ditch well, I have stood in it many a time.' His faith he expressed thus, 'I bet my life on Christ—Christ crucified'. He took Jesus Christ quite literally which endeared him to the poor but was not always so popular amongst the more respectable churchgoers.

Once he was to tell a pious congregation in a beautiful and ancient parish church that sometimes he felt he would like to take a great sledgehammer and smash every stained glass window in the church. He would then go out and celebrate the Eucharist in a field with a tea-cup and plate. And he wrote, 'Nobody worries about Christ as long as he can be kept shut up in churches. He is quite safe there. But there is always trouble if you try to let him out.'

During Geoffrey's four years in Rugby he was entirely at home in the dirtiest of kitchens, and would sit for hours smoking and talking, or watching by a sick-bed. He was most at home with the down and outs and lodging house tramps. Of an evening he would often be found, wearing his cassock, in some sleazy pub singing *Nazareth* while half his audience felt within a power unfelt before. Such was his love of the poor he would give his money and the clothes off his back to those in need. Eventually his landlady made him give her all his money and would dole it out to him daily. She once bought him as a gift a warm overcoat, and was not over pleased when he returned to the house one day without it. That too had been given away.

In 1912 Geoffrey left Rugby in order to help his father in his Leeds parish. There Geoffrey married in 1914 and when his father died, the parishioners of St Mary's wanted him to take on the living. That was not considered a good idea. Three different parishes were offered to him; one of these was St Paul's, Worcester. Of the three St Paul's paid the least and the people were the poorest. Characteristically he asked his wife if she thought she could live in the vicarage and in June 1914 he became the vicar.

In his first letter to his new parishioners he wrote, 'My study is a place where anyone can come and talk and be sure of a hearty welcome. I am not going to try to please everybody. That generally means the sacrifice of principles upon the altar of popularity, but I do want to be a friend to everyone and the servant of all in Christ.' He was taken at his word. So many people wanted to see him that, for his own sake, his wife began to limit the time when her husband was available. One day in his parish he discovered an old man, an invalid, lying on a very uncomfortable couch for he had no bed. First Geoffrey brought a pillow from the vicarage, then a pair of sheets. A bedstead followed, piece by piece, but when Mrs Kennedy came home she found her husband defeated. True she was a bed the less, all but a mattress, which Geoffrey was unable to manage by himself. She helped him carry it to the old man's house.

On 28 June 1914 the Serb Gavrio Princep assassinated the heir to the throne of Austria in Sarajevo, thereby sparking off the train of events which led Britain, in defence of her ally Belgium, to declare war on Germany on 4 August. To the average Englishman it looked as though we were leaping, as befits our generous nature, to the defence of the little man. Certainly Geoffrey would seem to have held that view for in his September magazine he was exhorting every able-bodied man to volunteer for military service. He offered himself as a chaplain, but at the end of the war wrote, 'When I went I believed that the war would end to the benefit of mankind. I believed that a better order was coming for the ordinary man, and God help me, I believe it still. But it is not through war that this order will be brought about. There are no fruits of victory, no such thing as victory in modern war. War is a universal disaster and as far as I am concerned I'm through.'

He knew what he was talking about. He experienced the full horror of war including at least three periods of active service at the Front. He had suffered from asthma for years and the appalling conditions in the trenches resulted in many sharp attacks. He used to say they make him feel 'like a rat pulled by its tail through a hedge on a wet morning'. Whatever the conditions he insisted on sharing them all with the soldiers. He was gassed and nearly blown up by a stray shell. During heavy fighting he tended the wounded and in one engagement, when the supply of morphia ran out at a dressing station, he volunteered to fetch some more. He had to dash from shell hole to shell hole across territory under heavy bombardment, but returned safely with fresh supplies of the pain-killer. After that he was out again, helping to bring in three wounded men. For that day's work he was awarded the Military Cross for 'conspicuous gallantry and devotion to duty'.

It is not surprising that such a priest was loved by the men. He once told a new padre who was anxious for advice about the 'job', 'Take a box of fags in your haversack and a great deal of love in your heart'. He might have been describing himself. The army had early given him the affectionate nick-name 'Woodbine Willie', those being the brand he constantly handed out, and like his tramps in Rugby or the poor in Worcester, they knew he loved them.

The military authorities made full use of his elo-quence; he must have been one of a very few chaplains who could hold the men's attention. It was during this time that he began to use his gifts of writing verse to preach the gospel in the Soldier's own language and the popularity of his poems in his life time and afterwards was enormous. Today we consider them rather sentimental, but then most of those for whom he wrote, appreciated that kind of poetry.

There was much talk among politicians of how social conditions were going to be much better after the war; Geoffrey was intensely concerned that they should be. When he left the army in 1919 he had become a very famous man. King George V had appointed him to be a Royal Chaplain and 'Woodbine Willie' was known to everybody. He was still Vicar of St Paul's but his heart had strayed from parish work. He had always served the poor as far as he could, now as a well-known figure, holder of the MC and a preacher who could pack any church he wanted to, he used his influence to proclaim 'the sacred cause of social justice' as William Temple was to put it. Inevitably Geoffrey was inundated with invitations to preach up and down the country. He became one of the speakers of a movement within the Church called the Industrial Christian Fellowship, a body dedicated to Christian Socialism. One of its tasks was to bring home to Church people their obligation as Christians for the social order in which they lived. Another was to send out lay missioners drawn from industry who, after special training, would be sent to bear witness to Christ in factories, on street corners, or wherever they could find people willing to listen.

Soon after his appointment to the ICF he left Worcester to become Vicar of the London City Church of St Edmund, Lombard Street. Apart from Sunday services there were few duties, and he was able to give nearly all his time to the ICF. He used however to preach twice a month in his own church and yet again crowds came to hear him. A high proportion of any congregation would be men and women who were unsure of their faith. He used to say 'When a man tells me he has no religion I simply take it that he is talking nonsense and proceed to find out what his religion is—what is it that gives life meaning to him. What one generally discovers is that a man or a woman has a god, but a poor one. And because he has a poor god, he is a poor person and is still in want, not knowing what he wants, but unhappy till he gets it.'

One morning early in March 1929 he left his home in Worcester a sick man. He was always travelling and for one of his constitution it was fatal. All his family were down with flu but he had one engagement in Liverpool. Some days later on 8 March he died in a Liverpool Vicarage. As his body was being taken across the Mersey ferry somebody quickly stepped forward and laid a packet of Woodbines on his coffin.

William Temple wrote of him, 'If to be a priest is to carry others on the heart and offer them with self in the sacrifice of human nature—The Body and the Blood—to God the Father of our Lord Jesus Christ—then Geoffrey Studdert Kennedy was the finest priest I have ever known.'

PRAYER: *Lord you give meaning to my life. Help me to be a friend to everyone and in Christ the servant of all.*

* * * * *

Oscar Arnulfo Romero   1917–1980

(24 MARCH)

'I am bound, as a pastor, by a divine command to give my life for those whom I love, and that is all Salvadoreans, even those who are going to kill me. If they manage to carry out their threats, from this moment I offer my blood for the redemption and resurrection of El Salvador.

'Martyrdom is a grace from God which I do not believe I deserve. But if God accepts the sacrifice of my life, then may my blood be the seed of liberty, and a sign that hope will soon become a reality.'

These words appeared in a Mexican journal, just two weeks before Archbishop Romero was shot at the altar of the Chapel of Divine Providence, as he was beginning to prepare bread and wine for the Eucharist, on 24 March 1980. It is a cancer hospital run by Carmelite nuns in San Salvador and Oscar Romero had made it his home since he had been appointed archbishop in February 1977.

San Salvador is the capital city of the smallest of the Central American republics, El Salvador, a country of only five million people, where since 1932 one dictatorship has followed another; and power resides in an oligarchy of about fourteen families, two of whom at least, if their surnames are anything to go by, must have originated, presumably in the nineteenth century, from Great Britain.

Romero himself was born in the town of Cindad Barrios, east of the capital and ten miles from El Salvador's northern neighbour, Honduras. His father worked for the Telegraph company but the boy left school when he was twelve to begin an apprenticeship to a carpenter. He proved to have the makings of a craftsman, but when a new and younger parish priest came to their church, Oscar was encouraged to consider ordination. His father was none too keen but grudgingly he allowed the lad to enter a junior seminary. Oscar completed his theological studies and training in Rome, but by this time Europe was engulfed in the Second World War. No member of his family therefore was present when he was finally ordained priest in 1942.

He returned to his country to work as a parish priest in Anamoros, but the ecclesiastical authorities quickly realised his potential as a Christian leader. In those days he was regarded as somewhat of a rigorist and among other jobs he was given successive charge of two seminaries.

One of the fruits of the Council of the Roman Catholic Church known as Vatican II was the setting up of local Episcopal Conferences. In 1966 Father Romero became secretary of his own country's Bishops' Conference and a year later secretary to the wider Episcopal Conference of the Central American isthmus.

In the meantime there had been growing up among Christians in many of the rural areas of El Salvador groups of people who were to become known as Base or Basic Communities. They had in common a fervent desire to follow out the implications of the Gospel more closely and they engaged in study, worship, group discussion and, when they recognized social needs in their midst, worked together to provide an answer to those needs. Each community had its own priest, many of whom were young Jesuits, together with a catechist and lay-ministers, who conducted weekly celebrations of God's Word. These leaders had been chosen by the groups, themselves and the sight of uneducated peasants choosing their own spokesmen alarmed the local landowners. In El Salvador 35% of all the good arable land is owned by a tiny percentage of the population. In other words over a third of the best land is owned by about 2,500 people. The Jesuits and others, now actively preaching Liberation Theology, which took as its basis the truth that God is on the side of the poor, were accused of Marxism and virulent campaigns were conducted against them in the press, while right-wing gangs began active persecution and killings.

Romero in 1970 had become Bishop, serving first as an assistant bishop to the ageing Archbishop of San Salvador and then in 1974 moving to Santiago. He was regarded by both the church and state authorities as being safely orthodox who could be relied upon to bring the Marxist priests and their Base Communities to heel and so the obvious choice to succeed to the Archdiocese of San Salvador. In February 1977 he became Archbishop and immediately set about gaining the confidence of his clergy, some of whom, quite naturally, were wary of him, They had worried unnecessarily. He knew that the cause of unrest in the country were 'a nucleus of families who don't care about the people. . . . To maintain and increase their margin of profits they repress the people'.

The civil authorities were particularly enraged by a Father Rutilio Grande in Romero's diocese; a Jesuit who was parish priest in Aguilaries, an area to the north of the capital. Rutilio denounced the injustice of a system which permitted a few to dominate and exploit the many. It was a district where 30,000 peasants lived, most forced to work on the thirty-five sugar-cane farms, or haciendas to give them the local name, in the season, and otherwise scratch a living from the remaining hill-sides. Defending him, Romero replied, 'The government should not consider a priest who takes a stand for social justice, as a politician, or a subversive element, when he is fulfilling his mission in the politics of the common good'.

Not two months after his enthronement, Romero was summoned to Aguilaries to view the body of Father Rutilio and the bodies of his two companions, a boy and an old man, all of whom had been shot, if not by the security forces, then by killer bands supporting the government. Nine days after the murder there was only one Sunday Mass celebrated in the diocese of San Salvador. All others had been prohibited by the Archbishop who instead had invited his flock to join him at the Cathedral on that day. The government were furious, but Romero refused to change his mind. 'It was a marvel,' wrote someone who had been present on that Sunday morning, 'to see the huge multitude of the faithful in the plaza in front of the Cathedral. The people understood the gesture and felt strengthened'. The Archbishop was making it perfectly plain to the rich and powerful of El Salvador that he believed that God was on the side of the poor.

By now Romero was determined to destroy any

lingering suggestion that the Church was a power which supported the state. In a Pastoral Letter to the Church and the Nation which he published for the National Festival on 6 August (the Feast of the Transfiguration of the Lord) he wrote, 'As long as the Church preaches eternal salvation without involving itself in the real problems of our world, the church is respected and praised and is even given privileges. But if it is faithful to its mission of denouncing the sin that puts many in misery, and if it proclaims the hope of a more just and human world, then it is persecuted and slandered and called subversive and Communist.' He took no part in any ceremonies, civil or religious, where Church and state might be seen as partners in government. It was the people he said, and not the church who had problems with the power of the state, and that explained the clash of church and state. 'The Church is not the Kingdom of God, but the servant of that Kingdom.' At the same time he vigorously condemned what he called 'the mysticism of violence'.

Violence was not the sole prerogative of the state or its agents. Not all of those who wanted change desired to see it brought about peacefully. In some areas peasants had seized land, giving the wealthy grounds for their fear of the masses. The military government by its very nature was unable to tolerate opposition of any kind. A frequent slogan appeared on the walls, 'Be patriotic: kill a priest!' After yet another change of government by a military take-over, in October 1979, guerilla activity increased despite Romero's constant appeals that Civil War should be shunned. A huge demonstration was organised for 22 January 1980 to commemorate and celebrate a peasant revolt of 1932. Security forces opened fire on the crowds, leaving twenty dead and over a hundred badly injured. Romero protested at the slaughter of men and women who had, 'taken to the streets in orderly fashion to petition for justice and liberty'.

Two months later he himself was dead, shot just after he had delivered what was to be his last sermon. In it he had reminded his fellow worshippers, 'You have just heard in the Lord's gospel that we must not love ourselves so much that we refrain from plunging into those risks history demands of us; and that those wanting to keep out of danger will lose their lives. On the other hand, those who surrender to the service of the poor through love of Christ, will live like the grains of wheat that dies. It only apparently dies. If it were not to die, it would remain a solitary grain. The harvest comes because the grain of wheat dies. . . . We know that every effort to improve society, above all when society is so full of injustice and sin, is an effort that God blesses; that God wants; that God demands of us.'

PRAYER: *Liberation, Lord, embraces my whole being, including my openness to your goodness and truth. Let my faith in your freedom inspire all that I do.*

When Pope John Paul II and Robert Runcie Archbishop of Canterbury made their historic pilgrimage to Canterbury Cathedral together, they lit a candle in the Chapel of Modern Martyrs to commemorate Oscar Romero.

Martin Luther King   1929–1968

(4 APRIL)

In the earliest printed record of The Diet of Worms
(1521) Martin Luther concludes an answer to his
accusers with the rousing cry 'Here I stand, I cannot do
otherwise'. The words appear on his tomb and could
well have been inscribed on the grave of the American
negro who bears his name. Luther, if he actually said
it, was referring to his theological opinions as they
appeared in his books. If applied to Martin Luther
King the words would be a reference to his intense
belief that the Christian Way includes a political struggle against oppression, but always a non-violent
struggle. 'Do good to those who hate you,' he took
literally, and a few years before his death it was a
growing source of grief to him that many of his
followers in the campaign for the Civil Rights of
American Negroes were asserting that they could only
achieve their political ends by violence. Over and over
again during the last years of his life Martin Luther
King had to talk various pressure gangs, particularly
of young negroes, into accepting peaceful demon-
strations. 'Might is Right' has a fateful fascination,
especially for the young; and Church history through
the centuries reveals how rarely Christians have been
prepared to follow Jesus who would not even resist
crucifixion. Martin once described non-violence as 'a
courageous confrontation of evil by the power of love,
in the faith that it is better to be the recipient of
violence then the inflictor of it.'

Although Martin's home in Atlanta lacked for
nothing he was nonetheless descended from a slave
and still subject to the insults and racial discrimin-
ations that were the pattern of life for the negroes in

America, especially in the Southern States, the majority of whose white population clung to the conviction that negroes were a lesser breed of men, fit only for exploitation. And the authorities as well as shops, restaurants and other commercial enterprises ensured a pretty rigid racial segregation, to the point that once when Martin and a friend were to entertain two girls to a meal, the restaurateur refused to serve them and fired a pistol into the air pointedly declaring that he would kill for less.

As a teenager Martin at first wanted to be a lawyer, but at college he changed his mind and was soon his father's assistant minister at Ebenezer Baptist Church, Atlanta. His formal education continued and it was not until 1954 that Martin, with his wife Coretta whom he had met while they were both students in Boston, moved into their new home in the parsonage of a highly respectable Baptist Church with a congregation from able negro professionals in Montgomery, Alabama.

During the Civil War (1830–1865) Montgomery had been the first capital of the Confederate States who had wanted to secede from the United States because the Federal Government was showing signs that it would abolish slavery. The Confederacy was short lived and the slaves given their freedom, but the state laws of Alabama were aimed at keeping white and black completely apart with the whites having all the advantages.

Fifteen months after his arrival, almost by accident, Martin found himself the leader of the negro citizens of Montgomery. A Mrs Rosa Parks began it all on 1 December 1955. She was on her way home from work tired and her shopping bag was full. She boarded a bus and dutifully went to sit on the hard wooden seats at the back of the bus. White passengers only sat in the front. The bus was full, and every seat taken so when the driver ordered Rosa to give up her seat to a white man who had just got on, she refused, was arrested and charged with an offence under the state segregationist laws. It was the last straw. Martin offered his church building for a protest meeting and within a week a negro boycott of the buses had been organised which was to last for over a year, only coming to an end when the US Supreme Court declared that segregation in buses was against the American Constitution. During the campaign Martin went to gaol, his family were threatened and insulted, and his home bombed. On that particular evening Martin was at a meeting but he rushed home and having first assured himself that his wife and daughter were safe he stood outside his wrecked porch and began to talk to the angry crowd that had collected there. They were in an ominous mood but Martin reminded them of the words of Jesus recorded in Matthew's account of his arrest in Gethsemane. 'All who take the sword die by the sword' (Matt. 26.52 NEB). Martin continued 'We must love our white brothers, no matter what they do to us. We must make them know that we love them. Jesus still cried out across the centuries "Love your enemies". This is what we must live by. We must meet hate with love.'

Such was the creed by which Martin directed a movement that rapidly spread throughout the United States. To begin with he and his followers protested within the context of the law, but in Birmingham, Alabama, Martin quite deliberately broke the law refusing to obey an injunction of the courts. Again he was gaoled and from his cell he addressed a letter to all the Christian leaders of the city invoking the maxim of St Augustine 'An unjust law is no law at all' in answer to their accusations that his movement's peaceful but

very large demonstration had been 'unwise and un-
timely'. 'I am in Birmingham' he wrote, 'because
injustice is here.' This was 1963, and it was marked by
the beginning of the passage of a Civil Rights Bill,
introduced into the American Legislature by President
John Kennedy and eventually passed by Congress
and signed by Kennedy's successor in 1964. Martin
was present at that historic moment.

On Wednesday 28 August 1963, a quarter of a
million people, over 75,000 of them white, converged
on the Lincoln monument in Washington in non-
violent demonstration. Martin was to deliver the final
speech and had been up most of the previous night
trying to get it just right. According to his wife, as he
came towards the end he abandoned his written
notes, and told this massive audience of his dream that
one day the United States would live out the meaning
of the words in the Declaration of Independence. 'We
hold these truths to be self evident, that all men are
created equal.' 'I have a dream,' he continued, 'that
one day on the red hills of Georgia the sons of former
slaves and the sons of former slave-owners will be able
to sit down together at the table of brotherhood. I have
a dream that one day the state of Mississippi, a state
sweltering with the heat of oppression, will be transformed into an oasis of freedom and justice.'

Martin spoke of freedom. 'When we allow freedom
to ring from evey town and every hamlet, from every
state and from every city we will be able to speed up
that day when all God's children, black men and white
men, Jews and Gentiles, Protestants and Catholics,
will be able to join hands and sing in the words of the
old Negro spiritual, "Free at last! Free at last! Great
God Almighty, we are free at last".' It was to become
his own epitaph.

In 1964 he was awarded the Nobel Peace Prize, and

on his journey to Norway to receive it called in at London to preach in St Paul's Cathedral. The theme of his sermon from the text 'its length and breadth and height being equal' (Rev 21.16 NEB) sums up his life's purpose. Martin spoke of the New Jerusalem which is God's design and concluded:

> 'Love yourself, if that means healthy self interest . . . That is the length of life. Love your neighbour as yourself; you are commanded to do that . . . that is the breadth of life . . . But never forget that there is an even greater commandment, "Love the Lord your God with all your heart, and with all your soul, and with all your mind." That is the height of life . . . God grant that we may move with unrelenting passion towards that city of complete life in which the length and breadth and the height are equal.'

Four years later Martin was assassinated in Memphis, Tennessee, a victim of a violent sick society. He was thirty-nine.

PRAYER: *Lord like you may I meet hate with love no matter what it costs.*

The United States now keeps an official Martin Luther King day.

* * * * *

Pandita Ramabai   1858–1922

(5 APRIL)

Although Ramabai was born into an orthodox Hindu family her father was a rebel who had insisted on teaching first his wife, then his daughter to read and speak Sanskrit. He belonged to the priestly caste, but nonetheless it was unheard of for a woman to be allowed to learn the sacred language. In fact he had to stand several trials before his Religious leaders before they acknowledged that nothing that he had done was actually forbidden in the Hindu scriptures. Many years later Ramabai proudly boasted, 'I am the child of a man who had to suffer a great deal on account of advocating female education, and who was compelled to carry out his views amidst great opposition'.

When she was twenty Ramabai astounded the Professors of Sanskrit at Calcutta by her knowledge of the language, but even then she had still not read the Vedas or the Upanishads, parts of the sacred scriptures which her religion taught her no woman ought to read. This is particularly strange in the light of her journeys at that time round Bengal and Assam, delivering lectures to crowded audiences on female education, for she shared her father's reforming zeal. She was desperately anxious to ameliorate the lot of women in her country, especially wives, who were considered their husbands' slaves and treated abominably. Much of her success is attributable to the fact that she constantly referred back to the ancient Hindu writings in her lectures, showing that the traditions that had grown up around marriage were far removed from Hindu doctrines. Her parents were dead and her companion on these journeys was her brother. Together they must have walked something like 4,000 miles. In 1912 Ramabai wrote and herself published her autobiography, a brief pamphlet which she entitled *A Testimony*. She describes the early journeys thus.

'I cannot describe all the sufferings of this terrible time. My brother and I survived and wandered about, still visiting sacred places, bathing in rivers, and worshipping the Gods and Godesses in order to get our desire. We had fulfilled all the conditions laid down in the sacred books, and kept all the rules as far as our knowledge went, but the gods were not pleased with us and did not appear to us. After years of further service, we began to lose our faith in them and in the books which held out the hope of a great reward to worshippers of the gods.' Although Ramabai forsook these gods and followed Christ, she never lost her intense devotion to Sanskrit.

She returned to Calcutta in 1878 and there met a Hindu, Kesab Chundala, a devotee of Christ, who like Gandhi, revered Jesus as a prophet but would not acknowledge his claim to be Son of God. Chundala introduced her to some Christians and she was given the Christian scriptures, translated into Sanskrit, but they made no immediate appeal to her. She married a lawyer in 1880 but two years later was a widow, with a baby daughter.

After the death of her husband Ramabai returned to her crusade for women and went to live at Poona. There she met some Anglican Nuns from the Community of St Mary the Virgin, usually known in Anglican circles as the Wantage Sisters after the little Berkshire town where they still have their Mother House. The sisters encouraged her to go to England for further education, and during her stay in England she visited a home for unmarried mothers in Fulham run by another Anglican Sisterhood. Her own words continue the story. 'I asked a Sister to tell me what it was, that made the Christians care for, and reclaim the "fallen" women. She read the story of Christ meeting the Samaritan woman, and his wonderful discourse on the nature of true worship, and explained it to me. She spoke of the infinite love of Christ for sinners. He did not despise them but came to save them. I had never read or heard anything like this in the religious books of the Hindus. I realised, after reading the Fourth Chapter of St John's Gospel, that Christ was truly the Divine Saviour he claimed to be, and no one but he, could transform and uplift the down-trodden womanhood of India, and of every land.

'Thus my heart was drawn to the religion of Christ. I was intellectually convinced of its truth on reading a book written by Father Gorch, and was baptized in the Church of England 29 September 1883 while living with the Sisters at Wantage.'

After her baptism and confirmation, Ramabai studied her newfound faith more thoroughly but was confused when she discovered so many different sects, each one claiming the authority of the same Bible for its particular theology. She goes on, 'I studied these different doctrines and made close observations during my stay in England and in America. Besides meeting people of the most prominent sects, the High Church, Low Church, Baptist, Methodist, Presbyterian, Friends, Unitarian, Universalist, Roman Catholic, Jews and others, I met with Spiritualists Theosophists, Mormons, Christian Scientists, and followers of what they call the occult religion.

'No one can have any idea of what my feelings were, at finding such a Babel of religions in Christian countries, and at finding how very different the teaching of each sect was from that of the others. I recognised the Nastikas of India in the Theosophists, the Polygamous Hindus in the Mormons, the worshippers of ghosts and demons in the Spiritualists, and the Old Vedantists in the Christian Scientists. Their teachings were not new to me. I had known them in their old eastern nature as they were in India; and when I met them in America I thought they had only changed their Indian dress, and put on Western garbs, which were more suitable to the climate and conditions of the country'.

This discovery so appalled Ramabai that when her book *The High-Caste Hindu Women* was published in 1877 she was beginning to lose her faith, and it was not until 1892 when she was back in India that she became an 'ardent and single hearted Christian'. Her book was, in effect, part of a campaign to raise money in America to start a home for high caste child widows. She raised the equivalent in dollars of 60,000 Rupees and an annual grant of 10,000 Rupees for ten years, and in March 1889 the home was opened at Chowpatty, Bombay, to be moved to new premises of its own in Poona eighteen months later.

By now Ramabai was something of a national figure in India. She avoided the mistake of many Indian Christians of behaving like a European after her conversion. All her life she wore Indian clothes and only ate food in accordance with the dietary laws of her caste, and she appeared on the political platform of the Indian National Congress to plead for the emancipation of women, and the plight of child widows.

Two years after the home had moved to Poona, as with John Wesley and so many Christians before and since, Ramabai's heart was strangely warmed. From that moment until the end of her life in 1922 she bound herself completely to Jesus Christ. In her anxiety to share him with the young widows in her caste she courted considerable criticism. She was accused of deliberately proselytizing, so much so that the authorities set up a special Hindu Widows' Home. Her own work prospered however and soon she was wondering how she could make her institution self supporting. A farm seemed the obvious answer and for two years she and a friend prayed that they might be able to buy sufficient land. The money came and she bought one hundred acres at Kedgoon. She began to clear the land, plant it with citrus fruit trees and have a well dug. It was ready just in time to help those stricken by a famine in the Central Provinces in 1896/97. Sixty women and a girl were rescued by Ramabai on her first tour of the famine areas and brought to live at Kedgoon. For four years she continued among the famine victims, often with her resources reduced to a few rupees, but God never failed her. When bubonic plague broke out at Poona and she had to evacuate the home and build a new home at Kedgoon she began without any funds at all, but every bill was paid. She never asked for a rupee, just fasted and prayed. In 1902 the work was extended to a boys' orphanage and before that a home for unmarried mothers.

Although Ramabai had begun her Christian life as an Anglican, the multiplicity of Churches and sects in the West convinced her that their divisions would never be reflected in her homes. As she grew older she used to spend longer and longer times in prayer, especially for the conversion of sinners. On one occasion in 1913 she had two vistors who arrived in the morning. They were told they could not see her. One of them describing the visit wrote afterwards 'We were told she was busy and I discovered later that she was all the time in meditation and prayer'. In 1905 she had begun an active career as an evangelist, going herself and sending out others to preach in the nearby towns and villages, and in the last years of her life she learned first Greek and then Hebrew so that she could translate the Bible into Marathi. She never lived to see it in print for she died in her room at Kedgoon on 5 April 1922.

PRAYER: *Lord lead me in your truth and teach me, For you are my saviour (Psalm 25.5).*

Pandita Ramabai's name appeared in a booklet 'Commemorable Names' issued by the Church of South India.

*   *   *   *   *

Dietrich Bonhoeffer   1906–1945

(9 APRIL)

'Jesus asked in Gethsemane, "Could you not watch with me one hour?" That is a reversal of what the religious man expects from God. Man is summoned to share in God's sufferings at the hands of a godless world.'

Dietrich was a very religious man, yet he is often thought of as one of the modern theologians responsible for extravagant theories concerning the 'Death of God' and for teaching ideas about religionless Christianity. The words quoted above are taken from a letter he wrote from Tegel Prison in Berlin to his close fiend Eberhard Bethge, then serving in the German army in Northern Italy. Dietrich himself was in gaol on suspicion of being involved in a conspiracy against Hitler and the central government of the Third Reich. This was true. He had been in touch with Allied Governments through his Church contacts, one of whom was the Bishop of Chichester in England, George Bell. The conspirators were anxious to discover what terms they could expect from the Allies should they be successful in their attempts to overthrow Hitler and his regime. 'Unconditional surren-der' the answer they received, did little to encourage them.

When he wrote that letter, Dietrich had already been in prison for over a year. Astutely he had been able to throw doubt on the charges against him, and the authorities were unable to prove anything. Of course his opposition to Hitler and the Nazi ideal was well known. He belonged to a section of the German Lutheran Church which had frequently attacked specific policies of the government, especially the anti-Jewish laws. He regarded his country's involve-ment in the war as unjust yet when war broke out he was himself in the United States and could have remained there. However, he deliberately returned to Germany in order that he might be totally identified with his nations's sufferings.

He had made his name as a Christian thinker and writer of some consequence before the War. Apart from his letters from prison, perhaps his most famous book is 'The Cost of Discipleship' in which he casti-gates the church for selling Christianity short. He calls it 'cheap grace', 'the preaching of forgiveness without requiring repentance, baptism without church disci-pline, communion without confession, absolution without personal confession. Cheap grace is grace without discipleship, grace without the cross, grace without Jesus Christ, living and incarnate.'

He nearly survived the war, but after a semblance of a trial he was hanged at Flossenburg on 9 April 1945. The camp doctor later wrote:

'I saw Pastor Bonhoeffer before taking off his prison garb, kneeling on the floor praying fervently to his God. I was most deeply moved. . . . In the almost fifty years that I worked as a doctor, I have hardly

ever seen a man die so entirely submissive to the will
of God.'

PRAYER: *God in your mercy bring us through these times,
but above all draw us to yourself.*

A Lutheran Church in Sydenham, South London is dedicated to Dietrich
Bonhoeffer.

*   *   *   *   *

Gemma Galgani   1878–1903

(11 APRIL)

On 8 June 1899, at Lucca, fifteen miles North East of
the famous Italian city of Pisa, there appeared, for the
first time, in the hands, feet and side of Gemma
Galgani marks similar to those of the wounds of our
Saviour. She thus joined that small band of Christians
who like St Francis of Assisi (1181–1226) the first of
their number, have been so devoted to Jesus on his
cross that they have wanted to share in his sufferings
as literally as they could. Since Francis over 300 people
have received *The Stigmata* as it is called, and sixty of
them at least have been declared saints within the
Roman Catholic Church; but it is well to remember
that no-one has been canonised simply on the
strength of such mystical or ecstatic experiences. 'With
faith, if it does not lead to action, it is in itself a lifeless
thing' (James 2.17 NEB). Holiness makes a saint, and
Gemma followed faithfully her own advice to her
sister 'striving only to be good'.

She was born at Camigliano on 12 March 1878. Her father was a chemist so Gemma and her family wanted for very little. She was an extremely clever child and devoted to her family, especially her mother from whom she learned her own love of Jesus. She grew up to be a vivacious but also a very self-controlled young woman and her straightforwardness sometimes made people think her rude.

None of her family, including Gemma herself, seems to have enjoyed very good health. Her mother bore eight children but only three survived. Signora Galgani died of TB when Gemma was seven, and an adored older brother when she was fifteen. Four years later her father developed cancer of the throat and died a bankrupt, leaving the remaining members of the family in penury.

During her mother's last illness Gemma was constantly in the sickroom, until the doctor issued instructions that everyone was to be kept away. Gemma was very distressed, and begged earnestly to be allowed back. When writing about it later she said 'Away from my mother, who would urge me to pray and to love Jesus?' The doctor relented and Gemma describes her return to her mother, 'I drew near to her, knelt by her pillow and prayed'. In her anguish at that early age, she was learning, as she later put it, 'how to love'. Her mother, guessing that her illness would be fatal, was anxious that Gemma should be confirmed before she died. Kneeling in church on her confirmation day Gemma became convinced that our Lord was asking her to surrender to him, even her love for her mother. After a struggle the little girl, who desperately wanted her mother to live, said yes to Jesus and ran home to find her mother dying.

As a young woman, and she only lived to be 25, she took as her motto *Jesus always*, although her mother's death had taught her that that can sometimes be very costly. At fifteen she herself became extremely ill and had to leave school. It was during that sickness that her brother died and Gemma was left to keep house for the diminishing family. She now spent hours in prayer, but whenever she could she would help the poor in her town. Anyone in need in Lucca knew that they would rarely be turned away empty handed from the front door of the Galgani household.

31 December 1896 saw Gemma making a tremendous New Year's Resolution. 'I have made up my mind to begin a new life. I don't know what is going to happen to me during the coming year, but I give myself completely to you, O my God. All my hopes and affections shall be for you. I feel my weakness Jesus, but I rely on your help. I resolve to live differently, that is closer to you.' Gemma kept that resolution, through her father's death and through the extreme poverty that for a while followed on it.

She had to face suspicion too from the church authorities when they heard of her mystical experiences, or else the alternate scepticism or adulation of the public when they got to know about them. Added to all this was her constant ill-health, culminating in a long drawn out illness which ended in her death on Holy Saturday, 11 April 1903.

PRAYER: *Jesus I want to live differently: I want to live closer to you.*

Gemma Galgani was canonised by the Roman Catholic Church in 1940.

Toyohiko Kagawa   1888–1960

(23 APRIL)

Toyohiko was at school in Tokushima on one of the southern islands of Japan called Shikko. His step-mother who was not at all fond of him had nonetheless allowed an older brother to pay his fees at the school where Toyohiko was proving to be extremely clever. However in those days it was imperative for any ambitious Japanese lad to be able to read English and so Toyohiko went to a Christian missionary in the city for lessons. One of his text books was the New Testament and he began with St Luke's gospel. His English was not good enough for him to be able to read the entire book unaided, but one day his teachers told him how it ended and the story of the crucifixion shattered Toyohiko. He found it almost impossible to believe that Jesus, after having done so much for people, could have been killed. It drove the fifteen year old to his knees and he prayed 'Oh God, make me like Christ'. But he hesitated to ask for baptism. Toyohiko's older brother was dead and now an uncle was paying for his education. To become a Christian would probably mean the end of that. One day his Christian teachers challenged him. Ought he not to be baptized? Toyohiko explained his fears should he come out into the open, but the charge of cowardice that followed, not as a jibe, but as a plain statement of fact forced him to think again. He asked for baptism. When he told his uncle he expected to be thrown out neck and crop but his uncle didn't seem to mind.

By now Japan was at war with Russia. All available young men and older boys were compelled to take up military training. Toyohiko couldn't. He had taken to heart the words of Jesus 'Love your enemies' (Matt.

5.44). On their playing field, now a parade ground, Toyohiko allowed the rifle that had been thrust at him to clatter to the ground. He refused an order to pick it up and said he believed Japan was wrong in going to war. His teacher knocked him down, and continued kicking Toyohiko in the face and stomach until he could kick no longer and the boy crawled painfully off the field. Two years later he was defying his uncle who wanted him to go to the Imperial University and thus enter politics. Toyohiko calmly told him that he intended to be ordained. This time he was thrown out.

He had first visited the slums of Tokushima with his Christian teacher while still living at his uncle's. In an evil-smelling alley he had been taken into a tiny hut and there welcomed by a young man who after his conversion to Christ had come to live in those sordid conditions to serve the poor as he believed Jesus would have done. A few years later Toyohiko used this young man's story as the plot for a novel. Of much greater importance, however, was the effect it had on his own thinking, and on Christmas Day 1909 Toyohiko himself went to live in the slums of Kobe at Shinkawa.

He was twenty one and had been studying for the ministry but becoming all the time deeply conscious of the gap between the official churches and ordinary everyday life. His lecturers seemed unaware of how the rest of the world lived, or how the poor suffered. Helped to move by an ex-convict, he set up home in a hut he had rented. It had been quite cheap because it had been the scene of a murder and the locals believed that the dead man's ghost still haunted the place. It was filthy inside but Toyohiko quickly set to work with a broom. At nightfall he sat in the dark, cross-legged on the floor, praying. He had no money for oil. Next day his neighbours were impressed to see him still alive and soon a young man covered with dermatitis asked to share his hut. On the following night a mentally distressed man came and on the next a drunk joined the household. Every morning Toyohiko rose before sunrise to say his prayers and by six o'clock in the morning he was standing at one of the street crossings preaching to all who would listen. He would spend the mornings at college and in the evenings he would be back in Shinkawa, preaching or just talking in his hut to those who came to him. He not only preached love, he lived it. 'I cling to men, I love them, I can't help loving them!' he wrote once. He suffered too at the hands of bullies, drunks, gamblers, brothel owners, but whenever he was attacked he never fought back.

Such work as his was bound to grow and consequently Toyohiko became quite famous. He married in 1914 and three months afterwards through the help of the churches he sailed for America to study at Princetown University where at the end of two years he had realised that simply trying to alleviate the lot of the poor was insufficient. What was necessary was a change in the law. The problems at the root of poverty had to be tackled.

To begin with Trade Unions were forbidden in Japan. Toyohiko saw their foundations as one of the most important tasks for the Church to initiate. Some of his fellow Christians were horrified. Surely that wasn't the job of the churches? He wasn't to be deterred, even when he was imprisoned for his activities in 1921 and again a year later. It was the government who gave in. While he was in prison he wrote two of the hundred and fifty books he wrote in all. One wonders how he found time for them. He was convinced that Christ was the only real answer to his country's and the world's problems. During the twenties and thirties he preached Christ in many cities, not only throughout Japan but also abroad. He had little time for theological differences and once told an audience in America 'I speak English very badly. When I say "denomination" some people think I am saying "damnation". I am not surprised. To me, they are very much the same thing.'

In 1940 he was arrested because during a visit to China he had apologised for the Japanese attack on that country. During World War Two he denounced first his own country and then America and her Allies for their pursuit of war. It was after the war that the Japanese Government asked him to help in the reconstruction of his country. Among other achievements Toyohiko was able to see all the Unions, which had been proscribed during hostilities, restored.

At about the time of a general election in 1946 the Emperor sent for Toyohiko. For nearly two hours, to the distress of court officials who had timed the visit for only thirty minutes, Toyohiko preached the gospel of peace to his sovereign. At the end of the audience, from his tattered bible, he had read to the Emperor, 'Who ever would be first must be the willing slave of all' (Matt 20.27). That had been Toyohiko's guiding principle all his life and remained so until his death on 23 April 1960.

PRAYER: *O God, make me like Christ.*

Abdul Karim   1906

(date unknown in MAY)

The border country between Afghanistan, Pakistan
and Kashmir used to be known in the days of British
Rule of the Indian sub-continent as the North-West
Frontier, and many are the stories of military exploits,
secret service missions and the like that have their
source in what is now the North West of Pakistan.
Pakistan is predominantly Muslim and it is a sad fact
that Christian teaching so far has made little headway
among Mohammedans. One reason is that to become
a Christian means being utterly rejected by one's
family, and thus it happened to Abdul Karim.

He lived at Quetta about 50 miles from the border
with Afghanistan and his father was an Islamic judge.
At Quetta a Doctor Sutton had founded a hospital for
the Church Missionary Society and through the hospital the doctor struck up a friendship with young
Abdul. When a boy, as might be expected with his
family background, Abdul had been deeply instructed
in the ways of Islam and knew the Koran, the Moslem
scriptures, very thoroughly. Jesus appears in the
Koran, but only as a prophet, and when Abdul and Dr
Sutton began to study the Christian scriptures
together, the more Abdul read, the more convinced he
became that Jesus Christ was more than a prophet. He
really was the Son of God.

At first Abdul hesitated in asking for baptism, for he
knew the inevitable consequences, and dreaded ostra-
cism from his family. He was by now married, and had
become a wealthy landowner, but at length he did
publicly acknowledge our Lord and was baptised. As
he had foreseen trouble started almost at once. To
begin with nobody would work for him or his family.

They were boycotted by all their neighbours, even attacked in their home, and threatened with death if they would not give up their faith in Christ. Soon Abdul was penniless and a job was found for him as an Evangelist in the hospital. Daily he spoke to the patients, and would often refer to passages from the Koran itself as he fearlessly explained the Christian Way.

One day he went with another doctor to a village some hundred miles from Quetta. The local mullah (Mohammedan minister) came to their camp and suggested a public confrontation with the Christians, the doctor and a priest both Englishmen, and Abdul. The mullahs obviously thought that they had a golden opportunity of ridiculing Christianity, but as the discussion developed they had reason to change their minds. Neither the doctor nor the priest were of much help, for although they could speak the language they were not sufficiently fluent to maintain a theological argument at any depth. Not so Abdul. He replied to objection after objection quoting at length from the Koran until the Mullah was thankful to escape when sunset called them to their prayers.

Abdul had one over-riding passion in his life, the hope of winning his own people for Christ. Once he trekked 400 miles from Quetta to Bannu as a Christian holy man. In that part of the world such men are called fakirs and they rely exclusively on the gifts of those they meet for their food. Wherever Abdul went he preached the gospel and frequently met with much abuse. He arrived at Bannu little more than a skeleton, but rejoicing that he had suffered such privations in the service of his Lord.

He still had one further ambition. He wanted to carry the gospel to the Muslim inhabitants of the neighbouring country, Afghanistan. Missionaries at

Quetta tried to dissuade him for they knew that very few Christians who had gone into Afghanistan as evangelists returned alive. One morning in May 1906 Abdul could not be found anywhere in the hospital. A week later the authorities in Quetta learned that one of their citizens had been arrested over the border and was in some distress. A message was sent to the Amir of Afghanistan demanding, his release. There was no response. It was Abdul. He had secretly crossed into the country, had been captured, and imprisoned in the city of Kandahar. Round his neck he had a chain weighing some seventy pounds. His feet too were manacled, his wrists handcuffed, and a bridle was thrust cruelly into his mouth. Later he was sent to the capital, Kabul, and there after urgent representations from the British Authorities it was agreed that he should be discharged. News of his imminent release from custody leaked out and he was seized by a crowd who gave him the choice of death as a Christian or his life if he would forsake Christ. He refused to deny his Lord, and they cut off one of his arms. Again they offered him his life if he would recant. Again he refused and his other arm was struck off. Yet again he was offered his life and a third time he remained steadfast, so they killed him.

Years later an Afghan who had seen him die told another Christian Missionary, 'I have never been able to forget it. In the streets of Kabul I saw him tortured and hounded to death for his faith. He was a Christian, so they told me to spit in his face, and they cursed him for an infidel, but the remembrance of the light and peace of Abdul Karim's face remains with me to this day'. It is very possible that this man too was later put to death for his Christian faith. Certain it is that another Pathan Nasrullah Khan, this time an Afghan national who also worked at Quetta Hospital was in

August 1908 himself killed by his own nephew because he would not deny Christ.

PRAYER: *Father, my cares and my hopes I place in your hands; help me not to worry about myself or my future (Edith Stein)*

The names of Abdul Karim and Nasrullah Khan appear in The Book of Anglican Modern Martyrs, St Paul's Cathedral, London.

$$* \quad * \quad * \quad * \quad *$$

William Edwin
Robert Sangster   1900–1960
(24 MAY)

A young conscript in the British Army was kneeling by his bunk in the barracks, saying his prayers. He did it every night but that evening a mate brought the flat of a bayonet smartly down on the soldier's backside. Heedless of the Lord's command the young Christian sprang to his feet and knocked his tormentor to the other side of the room with one blow. William Sangster found it hard to forgive himself for re-acting so violently. 'Yet I have always suspected,' his son Paul wrote many years later, 'the real sin in my father's eyes was the fact that he relished that blow all his life.'

Will had joined the army just at the end of World War I. He was sent to Germany in the army of occupation and even hoped for a commission but the officers had no intention of allowing a 'Holy Joe' as they called him into their mess. He remained an NCO until he was released to begin training for the ministry in the Methodist Church, into which Ministry he was ordained at York on 27 July 1926. In the same year he married the girl of his choice whom he had first met when he was 16, and together they set up home in the Manse at Conway, North Wales, where Will had been appointed Minister. Such was the humble start to a career that was to rocket twenty-five years later to the supreme place in English Methodism, President of Conference.

During the Second World War the cellars of his church in London, Central Hall, Westminster, became air raid shelters. Thousands of people who would not have dreamed of going to a service there, crowded into the basement. As for John Wesley, the world became Will's parish and he dearly wanted to share Christ with them, but he was quite certain that the secret of power over the unchurched multitude was supernatural love, 'quite free, as far as humans can have it, of any ulterior motive. It is no good loving them for anything except themselves. Not even for Church, prayer, goodness. If you do they see through you. It must be just God's love in you, even though all the signs seem to show they prefer the devil.' Later when he was returning from one of his many and successful tours abroad he wrote 'Nothing matters much in this world but to be a channel of God's love'.

It was the pastoral work, loving men and women into God, that he missed most when he was elected by the Methodist Conference of 1955 to become Secretary of the Home Missions Department. He delighted most in serving people like Jessie who had been one of his flock at Aintree in Liverpool. Once when she was in hospital Will visited her.

'Mr Sangster,' she said, 'God is going to take my sight away.' Will remained silent for a moment then said, 'Don't let Him Jessie. Give it to Him.' 'What do you mean?' replied the girl. 'Try to pray this prayer,

"Father if for any reason I must lose my sight, help me to give it to you".'

During the last months of 1957 Will knew that he was ill, but said nothing. Later in that year the muscles of his whole body began to twitch and his throat felt tight. By September of the following year it was clear to the doctor that Will was developing muscular atrophy, a condition for which there is no known cure and in which the sufferer gradually loses all his muscle power until even the throat muscles cannot function. Jessie had only to give her sight to God, for Will it was his life. His body slowly collapsed but he was able to write in the diary that he began to keep in 1959. 'It is love and mercy all the way.' He used his enforced hours of idleness well, 'Praying in love and faith for other needy people is one sovereign way I use; not just (God help me) for the "pay-off" to myself, but out of a deepened sympathy for all who suffer.'

His illness lasted for two and a half years. Always a devoted son of the Founder of Methodism, he died almost as if he had planned it, on Wesley's day, 24 May 1960.

PRAYER: *Father, if for any reason I must lose any of my senses or my faculties, help me to give them to you.*

Thomas Walter Bako   c 1856–1902

(3 JUNE)

To be sold into slavery at six years old is not a very promising start to life but Thomas was lucky. He had been captured when men of the Nupe tribe attacked his native village of Okomatonigi in Nigeria, but was later redeemed by a Church Missionary Society priest and went to live in the Mission Station at Lokoja. Instead of the life of a slave he went to the Christian school and within the year had asked for baptism. He was obviously quite a bright youngster and the missionaries eventually sent him on for further education at a Training Institute in the capital city, Lagos. He was married before he went to college and while at college confirmed. Two years later in 1883 he was appointed by the Church Missionary Society as school master at Kipo Hill, an outpost of the Lokoja Mission, at a monthly salary of thirty shillings. Two others were appointed at the same time but he seems to have been the only one satisfied with the salary offered! He must have been a conscientious teacher for a year later he had been recommended as an assistant catechist, a kind of lay-reader, with an increase of salary.

In 1886 Thomas was transferred to the school at Kokoja and there he played an active part in the Church. He helped in the translation of the Psalms for a Common Prayer Book in the Nupe language and was popular among his own people, though he sometimes did not take too kindly to those in authority over him.

During his years at the Lokoja school he began to wonder if he might offer himself to Bishop Tugwell of Nigeria for ordination. He approached CMS about this in 1896 but at that time the Society and the Bishop were unable to accept him. A year later however he was appointed senior Catechist and went to work at yet another outpost of the Lokoja Mission at Ghebe. Here and at Akube he was a great influence for good, especially among the men of the villages, and in 1900 was chosen, chiefly as an interpreter for he spoke eight native languages, to accompany the Bishop on a tour in the area. During that tour, as the Bishop later wrote, 'Dear Bako practically saved our lives when we were all so ill at Gierko. He nursed us day and night until he too fell ill'.

In 1902 the Missionaries at Lokoja decided on a plan to reach out to other villages who had not yet heard the good news of Jesus Christ. Thomas and three companions, a fellow catechist called Obegha and two school boys, set out from Lokoja in order to travel towards Kotou Karifi, travelling up the Niger to meet an English priest John Aitken who also came from Lokoja. Part of that priest's own letter continues the story.

'Bako heard that the road was not quite safe but thought he would attempt it as he had no loads excepting food and bedding with a few things to be used as *dashes* (that is gifts for barter). An attack by robbers under such circumstances he thought, was out of the question. Unfortunately they were attacked by some ten Hausa-speaking robbers armed with arrows and swords. Bako wanted to explain who he was but both he and Obegha were shot with poisoned arrows, Obegha in the neck by a blunt one which just buried the head in the skin but could not pierce the throat, and Bako through the muscle of the thigh just above the knee joint, preventing his running away. Obegha ran into the bush while Bako told the boys how and where to run. They went into the bush and hid after out-running their pursuers, one of whom tripped and fell. The robbers then attacked Bako with swords and gave him some terrible wounds. He fell down and feigned death whilst they beat him with sticks, and stripping him of most of his clothes, left him for dead.' John Aitken then goes on to explain how the boys got help. In a journey of great suffering Thomas was eventually brought back to Lokoha only to die of blood poisoning through the wounds received in His Master's service a few days later on 3 June 1902.

PRAYER: *Be not far from me, Lord, for trouble is near and I have no-one to help me (Psalm 22.11).*

Thomas Walter Bako is commemorated in his own parish and diocese and his name appears in the Book of Modern Anglican Martyrs in St Paul's Cathedral, London.

The author is grateful to CMS for permission to print part of the letter of the Revd John Aitken from their archives.

* * * * *

James Hudson Taylor 1832–1905

(3 JUNE)

He was nearly eighteen, and convinced that God wanted him to preach the Gospel in China. He knew very little about that country and a friend in Barnsley, where he worked in his father's chemist's shop, had told him that a local Congregationalist Minister had among his collection of books the then standard English work about China. James called on the clergyman hoping to borrow the book and when he was asked why he said he thought God was sending him to China.

'And how do you propose to go there?' asked the clergyman. 'I don't know at all. It seems probable that I shall need to do as the Twelve and Seventy did in Judea. Go without purse or scrip, relying on him who is sending me, to supply all my needs.'

The minister smiled indulgently and placed his hand on James' shoulder 'Ah, my boy,' he said, 'as you grow older you will become wiser than that. Such an idea would do very well when Christ himself was on earth but not now'. James knew only one way of treating such advice. He ignored it.

His own Wesleyan Church had no missions in China, although a Dr Charles Gutzlaff had founded *The Chinese Association* to send native Chinese Christians into the interior of the country. In the nineteenth century most missionary work was restricted to a few coastal areas, though two centuries earlier Jesuits had actually penetrated to the Imperial Court and been favourably received. It is one of the scandals of Christian disunity that in the nineteenth and early part of this century it is hard to believe that Catholics and Protestants worshipped the same God or followed the same Christ. Neither had a good word to say for the other.

James contacted the London Headquarters of the Chinese Association, but in 1851 he moved to Hull to become assistant to a Dr Hardey. For a while he lived with his employer's family but then moved into a single room of his own in a poorer part of the town. He had been accustomed to visiting the poor in their homes, now he lived and worked among them, sharing their lot as fully as he could. As he himself later wrote, he had wanted to accustom himself to endure hardness and economise 'in order to be able most largely to assist those amongst whom I spent a good deal of time labouring in the Gospel'. He lived extremely simply and was thus able to give away two thirds of his salary.

His life, when he left Hull for London in order to train as a doctor, makes fascinating reading. He lived on brown bread and water with apples for lunch, survived a malignant fever, and never lost his burning conviction that God meant him to go to China. Six years after he had, as his mother was to put it, heard our Lord say 'Go for me to China', James landed at Shanghai. He might have chosen a more propitious time for the country was in the throes of civil war, and Shanghai was soon to be under seige. At the end of the year he had set off with a fellow missionary on his first journey through the interior. Nearly a year later and after six further journeys, he came to a momentous decision. He would cease to live as a European; he would adopt Chinese dress and have his head shaved in the current native fasion, leaving only enough of his curly hair to grow into a pigtail. He first appeared in the gown and satin shoes of a 'Teacher' on 24 August 1855 and set out on his eighth missionary journey. Dressing as a Chinaman was no gimmick. He wanted to live in the same way as those to whom he had come to preach the Gospel. He was even married in his new style clothes on 20 January 1858 and he and his wife Maria set up house in Bridge Street, Ning-Po, as the crow flies over a hundred miles due south of Shanghai. In October of the following year James found himself having to take on the running of a Christian Hospital, the work of a Dr Parker who had had to return to Scotland.

As soon as James assumed responsibility for the hospital he called a meeting of all the staff. He told them that he had enough cash in hand to keep them going to the end of the month. Thereafter he could not guarantee to pay anybody's salary. Those who were prepared to stay, relying on God to provide their needs, must stay. Anyone who wished to leave to look for more secure employment could do so. All but the Christians left and James turned to local Chinese Christians to take their places.

The money left by Dr Parker was soon running low. James would not run into debt nor would he appeal for funds and when the cook appeared with the news that they had opened their last bag of rice, James simply replied, 'The Lord's time for helping us must be close at hand'. Before the bag was quite empty he had received fifty pounds, in those days a very tidy sum of money, with a request for details of how he could use more. The work prospered, the church grew and more helpers became essential. In a letter to his parents in January 1860 James wrote, 'Do you know any earnest devoted young men desirous of serving God in China, who, not wishing for more than their actual support, would be willing to come out and labour here?' Letters were insufficient and when James became quite ill he and his wife returned to England. He resumed his studies in medicine and they set up house with at least one Chinese Christian in Whitechapel. At the same time, with a CMS Missionary, they were engaged on a revision of the New Testament in the Ning-po dialect. A few men and women had offered themselves for work at Ning-po when they heard about the Mission, but James was concerned that Christ should be proclaimed throughout China.

All his life he trusted God to provide for his needs, down to the smallest details, but during a brief weekend with friends by the sea he pencilled in his bible 'prayed for twenty-four willing, skilful labourers at Brighton, 25 June 1865,' and two days later, relying on God's answering his prayer, he was opening a bank account for the *China Inland Mission*. In a pamphlet to launch the Mission he wrote: 'Our great desire and aim is to plant the standard of the Cross in the eleven provinces of China and in Chinese Tartary'. There followed hectic months which involved much travelling round the country, but in May 1866 with a party of sixteen missionaries and four children he and his wife sailed for China. Mrs Taylor would never see England again, she died four years later and in a wonderful letter to his mother soon after Maria's death, James writes that he will have 'to walk a little less by feeling, a little less by sight and a little more by faith'. He was separated too from his children, for they had been sent back to England some time before Maria's death.

Within six years of his return with those sixteen new colleagues, the CIM numbered thirty European missionaries and fifty Chinese, working from thirteen central stations at an average distance apart of one hundred miles. James had oversight of them all and his time was spent between them. In 1872, exhausted, he returned home again only to discover that he now had to take over the affairs of the Mission in England. It wasn't long before he was back in China and had stepped up his demands. In his Bible appears this note,

> 'Tai-chow 27 January 1874. Asked God for fifty or a hundred additional native evangelists and as many foreign superintendents as may be needed to open up the four Fu's and forty-eight Hsitus; also for the men to break into the nine unoccupied (he meant unoccupied by Christians) provinces. Asked in the Name of Jesus.'

The man who wrote 'Want of trust is at the root of almost all our sins and all our weaknesses . . . The man who holds God's faithfulness will dare to obey Him, however impolitic it may appear', relied utterly on that faithfulness and by 1876 his prayer for extra workers had been more than answered. In another six years, inspired by his work, CIM began to pray for a further seventy workers and James sent a telegram to the Mission's office in London asking them to receive and send out that number. In 1887 he was praying for a further hundred new missionaries. They came. One hundred and two to be exact.

He was now back home, stomping round the country to appeal not for money (he never asked for funds) but for men and women to offer themselves for service in China. He travelled back by way of the United States and Canada for a three month tour of churches there. Further visits to America followed and to Sweden, Germany, Australia, New Zealand and India. There was also a great conference of Protestant Missionary Societies working in China, from which went out an appeal for a thousand new workers over the following five years.

In 1900 James returned to London for the last time. On his journey to England he had heard the first news of the Boxer Rising. It almost killed him, he could scarcely cross his room unaided. When things were at their worst during August he said, 'I cannot read, I cannot think, I cannot even pray, but I can trust'. Thousands were killed, including fifty-eight of his missionaries besides twenty-one of their children. He longed to go back to China, but in the summer of 1901 he finally abandoned all hope of ever returning there to work. His health forbade it. But he died in China. He went for a visit during the first half of 1905 and died at Changa-Sha on 1 June.

PRAYER: *Father I cannot think; prayer is hard; but I can trust you.*

Angelo Giuseppe Roncalli
(Pope John XXIII) 1881–1963

(3 JUNE)

Pope John XXIII died on 3 June 1963. He had known he had an inoperable cancer for some time. When his doctors told him their diagnosis his response was typical of the man, 'Very well, let God's will be done. Don't worry about me, because my bags are packed. I'm ready to go.' During his last painful days on earth one prayer had been constantly on his lips. He took it from the high priestly prayer of Jesus on the night before he died. 'Ut unum sint,' (that they may be one. John 17.22). Those words sum up the life's work of Pope John, who once told an Anglican priest, 'Whenever I see a wall between Christians I try to pull out a brick'.

On 15 August 1905 when the newly ordained Angelo returned to his native village of Sotto il Monte, about eight miles from Bergamo in north Italy and not so very far from Lake Como, his family and friends were anxious to congratulate him. In those days it meant much to a peasant family when one of its sons was ordained priest. When he celebrated Mass in his family parish church they would all try to be there and afterwards someone was bound to call out, 'Now you must work hard and become Pope'. Never in their wildest dreams would they think it a real possibility that a man from a comparatively poor family might rise to such heights. In any case they knew Angelo. At school he had never been excessively brilliant, he had an irrepressible sense of humour, and certainly could never take on the suitably ascetic lean and hungry look.

His first job as a priest was near home. He became secretary to the newly consecrated Bishop of Bergamo, Giacomo Radini-Tedeschi. In those days he was considered a progressive bishop, being more concerned with the impact of the gospel on social conditions than in preserving the rights of the church. When the ironworkers of Ranica went on strike in 1909 over Union recognition, he and Angelo supported them publicly and helped to organise relief for the men and their families. The Bishop died in August 1914 but, before Angelo could find new work, World War I broke out and he was called back for service in the Italian Army. At that time no exceptions to the call-up were permitted, so that Angelo had had to serve a year in the army prior to his ordination. He had gained his sergeant's stripes and so returned to work in the Military Hospital at Bergamo as a hospital orderly. In 1916 the Italian Government allowed Chaplains to be appointed and it was as such that Angelo served for the remainder of the war.

In 1918 he opened a student's hostel in Bergamo but it was not long before he was summoned to Rome to be an official of the body designed by the then Pope, an old friend of his late Bishop at Bergamo, to unify Catholic Missionary work throughout the world. It involved much travelling but in 1925 he was consecrated bishop himself and sent as the Pope's personal representative to Bulgaria where most of the Christians belonged to the Orthodox Church. Angelo set about improving relations between the Orthodox Christians and those who adhered to his own Church. He was bitterly deceived by the ruler, King Boris, but when he left Bulgaria nearly ten years later they were extremely sorry to see him go to his new job as Apostolic Delegate to Istanbul.

Constantinople, the old name of Istanbul, was the

home of the spiritual leader of all Orthodox Christians, the Oecumenical Patriarch. Before 1054 the Church based at Rome and that at Constantinople had preserved some sort of unity though they often fell out. However in the eleventh century the Pope tried to enforce the customs of the Western Church on Eastern Christians who lived in Southern Italy. As a reprisal Western style Churches in Constantinople were all forcibly closed and on 16 July 1054 the Pope excommunicated (that is, cut off from the Sacrament) the Patriarch of Constantinople and all his followers. Eastern Christians for a long time before that had disputed Papal claims of authority over the universal church: the Bull of Excommunication left on the High Altar of the Church of the Holy Wisdom in Constantinople was the last straw. The Patriarch in his turn excommunicated the Pope and his followers and so the schism between eastern and western Christians began. For centuries Orthodox and Roman Catholic Christians had little to do with each other at any official levels. It comes as no surprise to find Angelo visiting the Patriarch as soon as possible after his arrival in Istanbul. It was the first time a representative of the Pope had called on the Oecumenical Patriarch for nine hundred years. A quarrel that had lasted for so long could not be patched up in one visit but two years after Angelo's death on 7 December 1965 the Patriarch and Pope John's successor lifted the mutual excommunications.

During World War Two, Angelo was active in helping Jews to escape from German occupied Europe and in getting the Allies to lift their naval blockade to allow food to be sent to the people of Greece, but in 1944 he was ordered urgently to leave Istanbul and fly to France to become Papal Legate there. In Paris he horrified some of his fellow Catholics because he got on so well with the Soviet Ambassador. Again he was to remain at his post for nearly ten years and just before he left France to become Patriarch and Archbishop of Venice he was made a Cardinal and therefore a member of the Sacred College which among other responsibilities has the duty of electing a new pope. Angelo by now was 72 and would have been forgiven if he had thought about retirement, but not so. The amount of work he got through was incredible and his new flock loved him from the start. In a letter he called it 'the beginning of my pastoral ministry' and he seems to have made the most of every minute.

13 October 1958 saw his arrival in Rome for the Solemn Conclave of its college of Cardinals to elect a successor to Pope Pius XII who had died four days earlier. Angelo was 78 and in the normal course of events would surely never have been chosen, but after several ballots he was, and took the name of John. Everybody when they heard the news said the Cardinals had chosen him as a kind of caretaker, to keep things ticking over for the few years left to him. Maybe the gossips were right but in four years he changed the whole course of his Church and made the reunion of all Christians a real possibility in, God willing, the not too distant future.

Since 1929 the Pope had been nicknamed 'The Prisoner of the Vatican'. Pope John XXIII made it quite clear that he had no intention of remaining in prison. He loved people and wanted to be with them. During his first Christmas Day as Pope he visited a children's hospital in Rome, the next day he was in a Roman Prison talking to the prisoners and confiding to them (to the horror of the Vatican newspaper who omitted it from their report) that there had once been a gaol-bird in his own family. He liked to walk in his own garden at the Vatican but insisted on doing it even when there might be tourists around. 'Don't worry about it' he told his advisors when they remonstrated with him because the tourists might see him. 'I promise not to do anything that would scandalise them.'

On 11 October 1962 Pope John XXIII was at the rear of a procession of the world's Roman Catholic Bishops entering St Peter's. It was the beginning of the Second Vatican Council which John had convened to the consternation of a large number of Vatican Prelates and clerics. He wanted the Roman Church to take a fresh look at herself and the gospel she taught. Above all he looked forward to the day when the Christian Churches would no longer be divided. The Curia, as the authorities in the Vatican are sometimes called, had done its best to ensure the old ways should not be disturbed, but John himself made certain that the council would be free in its discussions. By calling the Council John knocked the wall between Christians down so far that they could shake hands with each other. The first session ended on 7 December 1962, and good Pope John was dead before the second began.

PRAYER: *Lord help us to follow all that leads to peace.*

* * * * *

Matthew Talbot   1856–1925
(7 JUNE)

'He was a terror for the drink; they all were.' Such was the opinion of the Talbots, especially of Matthew's younger brother Philip, held by one of their Dublin neighbours. Their mother and her eldest son John appear to have been the only stable members of the family.

Matthew, the second son, was born on 2 May 1856 and by the time he was twelve he was working in the worst of all possible situations for a Talbot—a messenger boy for a wine merchant and bottler. Inevitably Matthew learned to drink deeply but when at fifteen he came home drunk his father thrashed him, made him leave his job and sent him to work for the Port and Docks Board.

After three years he left the Docks to become a bricklayer's labourer. He was a good workman, so much so that his boss always placed him at the front of a gang to ensure that the others would be unable to shirk if they were to keep up with him. Matthew worked hard and drank heavily, even pawning his boots to get money for beer. He was paid on Saturday mornings and by the evening he would have spent out. One Saturday night he returned home in his bare feet and had only one shilling to give to his mother for his keep.

Matthew's house was a Christian one. Nobody in the family would dream of missing Mass on a Sunday and they prayed together at home as well. Even when he had come home drunk well past midnight on a Saturday, Matthew would be up next morning to go to Church. He was not prepared to ditch God completely. Unemployment and the appallingly crowded conditions in which the poor of Dublin were forced to live, explain at times even excuse the city's enormous number of drunkards. For a few hours and a couple of pence men and women could forget their squalid surroundings, but blotting out the miseries of poverty merely created new horrors and Christians of all denominations tried desperately to persuade those who were hooked on alcohol to pledge themselves never again to drink intoxicants of any kind.

On a Saturday in 1884 Matthew Talbot suddenly announced to his long suffering mother that he was going to take the pledge. His mother thought she knew her son and almost tried to dissuade him. As he disappeared through the door on his way to see a priest she called out 'Don't take it if you don't mean it' then added, perhaps almost under her breath 'May God give you the grace to keep it'.

God did. From that day until 7 June 1925 when he died Matthew never drank again. It was not easy. He had to keep away from all his old drinking companions. When they were in the pubs he was in a Church, although he often had to go into pubs to pay back the money he owed the Publicans for past drinking bouts. Not a single debt was left outstanding. He had changed his job and was working for a Timber Merchant, and usually went to work with his pockets empty. This was quite deliberate. About three months after his conversion he had fought a hard battle with himself first outside a public house, and then inside at the bar. As it happened he had had to wait a long time for service and by the time the barman turned to Matthew he had gone, his word kept. To avoid a similar struggle Matthew thereafter rarely carried any money with him.

During the whole of his boyhood he had been to school for little more than twelve months. And when he was a pupil he often played truant, but somehow he had left with the rudiments of reading. He never told anyone why he had signed the pledge, or what had turned him to our Lord, but the money that he used to spend on beer was either given away or else spent on Christian books. Over the years he built up a very wide library, surprising in one who had received so little formal education. Obviously in his reading he often came across words or phrases he did not understand. At that point he prayed to the Holy Spirit for wisdom. God never let him down.

It hurt Matthew when his workmates misused God's name, and should he hear anyone blaspheme he would silently and reverently raise his own hat. He spent hours in prayer, even finding a cubby hole in a shed at work. In between loads, when there was no work to be done, he would not hang around but go to the shed to say his prayers.

In 1913 there was a general strike in Ireland. Matthew was perplexed. He believed strongly that men had the right to a just wage and he approved of their taking action to get it, but on the other hand he was frightened of the bitterness that would be inflamed by a strike. In the end he refused to work along with all the others, but instead of joining the picket lines he stayed at home to pray for justice and peace.

Matthew was similarly troubled during the struggle for Irish Independence. He wanted his country to be free and disliked it when he saw young Irishmen joining the British Army in its fight against Germany in the 1914–1918 war. Nonetheless it distressed him when so many people were killed and he spent hours in prayer for them all.

In the spring and summer of 1923 he was twice in hospital. When he left he was very poor for he had had to give up his job. Just before Easter in 1925 he returned to his old work, where his employer and workmates made sure he was only given the light tasks. By now he was living in digs and his landlady was very anxious about him. She urged him to carry his name and address in his pocket in case he should be taken ill. 'What do I need with my name and address?' he asked. 'Won't God be with me when I die?' His pockets remained empty. On another ocassion he hadn't been feeling at all well. Somebody offered to sit up with him during the night. 'Nobody can keep me,' said Matthew, 'if our Lord wants me.'

He had lived close to God for just over forty years. Soon after his conversion he had begun to sleep on a plank of wood, with a hard block of wood for a pillow. The body that he had indulged with excessive drinking from his teens was now to be trained in self-control. He fasted a great deal too. 'It is constancy that God wants' he used to say and Matthew Talbot meant to be constant. On the morning of Trinity Sunday 1925 he dropped dead in a Dublin street on his way to Church.

PRAYER: *Lord keep me constant: constancy is what you want.*

Matthew Talbot's cause for canonisation was officially recognized at Rome in 1975.

* * * * *

Evelyn Underhill   1875–1941

(15 JUNE)

Evelyn Underhill once completed a lecture she was giving on *'Religion in the Twentieth Century'* by telling a fairy story, about a little dwarf who lived in a wood. He had a wheelbarrow and every day he gathered from the wood a barrowful of slugs and snails. He was on the whole quite content with his lot but there was just one thing lacking. He badly wanted to see the King of the World who passed through the wood early every morning making all things beautiful and new.

Apart from his wheelbarrow the dwarf had one cherished possession, a lovely green blanket which he had once picked up when it fell out of the Fairy Queen's chariot, and which he had not been able to help keeping for himself. It was often very, very cold in the wood at night, but wrapped in his blanket he was always so warm and cosy that he never woke up in time to see the King of the World. One day a Shepherd came to see the dwarf. He looked deeply into his eyes and after an embarrassing pause exclaimed, 'Haven't you seen the King of the World yet?' 'No', said the dwarf very humbly. 'I do want to, but somehow I can't manage it'. There was an even longer pause, the dwarf wriggled uncomfortably. Suddenly the shepherd said, 'I seem to see something that keeps you from the vision . . . something ra- a- a- ther like a little green blanket'. 'And then', continued Evelyn Underhill, 'began that terrible battle in his heart between wanting to go on being warm and comfortable in his blanket and his longing to see the King of the World.'

When she delivered that talk, Evelyn had for many years decided that the vision of God was of far greater importance than anything else in the world, and as she once wrote 'I see only too clearly that the only possible end of this road (she meant the road to God) is complete, unconditional self-consecration'. She went on to say that she didn't think she had the nerve, the character, nor the depth for such dedication. This proved to be untrue. Her whole life was one of deeper and yet deeper surrender to God.

She was born in 1875. Her father was a solicitor who later became a barrister, and spent as much of his spare time as he could sailing his yacht, usually accompanied by his wife and daughter. Evelyn was a very clever child and in 1904 had published her first book, a novel called *The Grey World*. Neither of her parents went to Church but Evelyn did and was confirmed at fifteen. For a while, after she had left school she was an agnostic but gradually returned to a belief in God, though by no means holding orthodox Christian views.

She was much drawn to prayer and in 1924 visited a retreat house at Pleshey in Berkshire. Many believers, and not only Christian believers, like to spend some time at least once a year being quiet with God. Some like to do this with other Christians and they call it 'going into retreat'. At a traditional retreat there is not much talking, except on the part of the conductor who will deliver two or three addresses to help the retreatants in their quite times with God. The conductor also makes himself available to the retreatants individually over the two or three days of the retreat so that if they want to they can discuss with him anything that is troubling them.

In 1924 it was most unusual for a retreat to be conducted by any layman, let alone a woman, but not so long after making her first retreat Evelyn was back at Pleshey as a Retreat Conductor. After her return to belief she had asked the man who was helping her in her spiritual life, Baron von Hugel, himself a very holy and humble man, what he thought God was wanting her to do. At Pleshey she soon discovered. There and elsewhere for eight years or more she conducted retreats, sometimes as many as eight a year. The retreat addresses were later published and some are still being reprinted.

One of the most attractive things about her is her down to earth common sense. To one of her friends who was in trouble she wrote 'Don't try to be too brave about it will you, because that isn't any use in the long run. I'm sure it is for our weakness and need of him that God loves us best.' Evelyn was able to lead countless men and women closer to God because she understood both the attractiveness of God in his absolute goodness, particularly as revealed in Jesus Christ, and the weakness of our human nature. She told a group of teachers 'Be sure that religion is never offered to the young, as primarily something which will be a comfort to them, or out of which they can get something for themselves. The real Christian is always a revolutionary, belongs to a new race and has been given a new name and a new song. After all, our Lord himself had to leave his work to twelve quite inferior disciples.'

Although married to a childhood sweetheart, Evelyn to her great sorrow had no children. But it left her free for her retreat work, talks and her writing. In 1935 she was asked to write a book on worship. She had earlier published one on mysticism and that had been very well received. It is hard to believe that such a scholarly woman was almost entirely self-taught; she had never been to University. *Worship* when it was finally published created quite an impression, and in 1938 the University of Aberdeen made her an honorary Doctor of Divinity.

Evelyn was too ill at the time to go to Scotland to receive her degree. For many years she had suffered from asthma and it was getting much worse. When the Second World War broke out she and her husband left London for a time. She was back living with friends in January 1941 and died in June the same year. The last few months had been very difficult for her but then she didn't expect it to be otherwise. 'Trusting God', she wrote in a letter to a friend not long before she died, 'must mean trusting Him through thick and thin.'

PRAYER: *Lord help me to trust you through thick and thin.*

* * * * *

Peter Lee   1864–1935

(16 JUNE)

Churches and Cathedrals are named after Saints; Religious Communities often have the name of their patron saint in their title; Hospitals and schools are frequently named after great Christians. The nineteenth century philanthropist, Lord Shaftesbury has an avenue named after him in London, but Peter Lee, the miner's son, who was himself a miner for the greater part of his life, has a town bearing his name. Peterlee Development Corporation was founded in 1948 to build a new town in Britian, about eight miles north west of Hartlepool and twelve miles south east of Durham. It will eventually have a population of 30,000.

All his life Peter loved Durham, especially its magnificent cathedral, and it was in Durham that he died but he is buried at Wheatley Hill, a nearby colliery town. Someone at the time said of him, 'It was just like Peter to come back and lie among his own'.

He was born in a small terrace house in Trimdon Grange, not far from the site of Peterlee. As a lad he never stayed in one place for long. The family was always on the move and one year they moved five times. His father was an extremely good workman, but of independent mind which meant he was constantly taking or giving offence at work and thus forced to look for fresh jobs, regularly. Perhaps too, his Romany blood made him incapable of settling down in one place for any length of time.

His son Peter, sixth in a family of eight children, shared his father's independent spirit and his wanderlust as well.

He followed his father into the mines, and when he was twenty-one sailed for America to spend just over a year there wandering from mine to mine. He returned to his native country in 1887, a 'devil-may-care, drinking, fighting man, with a certain fine strain running through him' as his biographer Jack Lawson puts it. He fell in love and in February 1888 married, a childhood friend Alice Thompson. Marriage did not help him to settle down and within a fortnight he was involved in a fight at the back of his local, yet his powers of leadership among miners was growing and in 1892 he was appointed a checkweightman by the miners of Wingate. His job was to check the weight of coal hewed to ensure payment of a just price by the owners. Checkweightmen were not employees of the company but of the miners through their Union and they were elected by the men at the pit.

Eight years after his marriage Peter was off again, this time to work in South African mines, but he was back after a year, a changed man. 'The gospels and his own inner wrestlings had given him greater knowledge of himself, increased his sympathy and understanding of men, intensified his sense of social wrong.' His wife when he married had been a devout Methodist, now Peter who up to now had been more a free-thinker became a Methodist too. Being a natural leader he soon became a prominent layman at the chapel in Wheately Hill. A young men's class grew up spontaneously around him, and soon he had been appointed a Local Preacher. From then until his death, he regularly took his turn in the Methodist Preachers' circuits in Co. Durham.

In 1902 he was back as checkweightman, this time at Wheatley Hill colliery. A year later he had also been elected as a Parish Councillor. In 1907 he was on the local District Council and in 1909 he was elected County Councillor. Today there is nothing very spectacular about an ordinary working man being elected to posts in local or national government. In Peter's day it was a most extraordinary event, and just after World War One when his county became one of the first to return a Labour majority on the council, Peter became its chairman.

In December 1919 his fellow miners through their union elected him as their agent, which meant he had to live in the city of Durham. Nothing could have given him greater delight. His work both as chairman of the County Council and as a union official left him little spare time, and yet he guarded his day of rest as jealously as he could. But he was no Pharisee. He would avoid all normal business affairs on a Sunday but in face of a pit disaster, or trouble at a colliery he would never hesitate to go whatever the day. And in Methodist churches throughout the county he preached the gospel of Jesus who had scorned the world's strong ones and given His great love to the obscure, the poor, the defenceless.

His party were elected out of office in 1922, but were returned to power three years later and Peter was back as chairman. As such he was in office during the great strike and the plight of his own people was continually in his mind, yet he remained serene and unflurried. In all his years on the county council he is best remembered for his concern that the county should have an adequate supply of water. One of the local Water Board's new reservoirs is dedicated to his memory.

In 1930 he was elected General Secretary of the Durham Miners' Association, and in 1933 President of the Miners' Federation, now known as the National Union of Mineworkers. A year later he resigned from the County Council, and on Sunday 16 June 1935, with the words of the twenty-third psalm on his lips, he died.

PRAYER: *Lord help me to love both you and my brother.*

* * * * *

Boxer Martyrs in China   1900

(27 JUNE)

No single event can satisfactorily explain the Boxer Rising in China at the beginning of this century. Among other things the Chinese were still smarting under the defeats inflicted on them by Westerners during the nineteenth century in two Opium Wars (wars fought so that European merchants could import opium into China). Resentment against the intrusion of foreigners was rife and with good reason. Native Chinese found little to distinguish European Christian missionaries from European merchants or the gunboats and soldiers that frequently accompanied them, and they were angered by the special privileges for Christians that had been constantly wrested from an unwilling but helpless government.

In 1899 the Governor of the Northern province of Shantung, Yü Hsien, was bitterly anti-foreign. He encouraged the formation of a quasi-religious organisation which, because of its special form of physical training and its descriptive name *I Ho Ch'nan* (Righteous Harmony Fists), very quickly gained from the Westerners the nickname *Boxers*. One of the Boxers' mottoes, which they inscribed on large banners, could be translated, 'By Imperial Command Exterminate the Church' and it is certain that the Dowager Empress did nothing to discourage them.

On 31 December 1899 Mr Brooks, sent out to China by SPG, was killed about fifty miles south west of Tsinanfu. By February and March 1900 over seventy Christians had been murdered and the killings were to go on through to September. Altogether it has been estimated that 30,000 Christians, European and Chinese, Roman Catholic, Orthodox and Protestant, died during the Rising. It is almost impossible to decide if their murderers killed them because of their allegiance to Christ, or because they represented in the Boxers' eyes, the foreigner and his religion. The governor, Yü Hsien, made his position quite clear however, when he issued a proclamation saying 'The European religion is wicked and cruel; it despises the spirit and oppresses peoples. All Chinese Christians who do not sincerely repudiate it will be executed. Let all Christians fear and obey! The Boxers will not hurt persons—it is this religion they hate.'

Whatever the political issues may have been—and the history of the West's relations with China at that time should make us all hang our heads in shame—there is no doubt that many Europeans who were killed, suffered because of their devotion to Christ. One of them, a Mrs Simpson, who was

beheaded along with her husband James on 9 July at
T'ai-yuen-fu, wrote in a letter to her sister-in-law,
after the first news of the Rising had been received in
Europe, 'You will see how dark our way is, but he is
a light. He has gone before, and in him is no darkness
at all. As I grow older I feel God's ways are best. Once I
believed it because he said it; now I believe it because I
have proved it.'

Another, Thomas Piggott, whose wife Jessie and
their young son William perished with him on 27 June
was preaching the gospel from the open cart to any
who would listen as he and his family were being
taken to their deaths. On the same day Edith Coombs
returned to a hospital building from which the Christians were fleeing because she wanted to rescue a little
Chinese girl patient. Edith was struck on the head
with an iron bar and when she staggered to her feet
was thrust back into the burning house.

Father Cesidia Giacomantonio having been
repeatedly stabbed and left in agony for twenty-four
hours while awaiting his death stroke prayed, 'Into
your hands Lord Jesus I commend my spirit. Do not
hold this sin against them.' And seven year old Jessie
Saunders, when she and her family were trying to get
to safety said to her mother as the party was being
stoned and beaten by a gang of Boxers, 'They treated
Jesus like this didn't they'. As a result of that journey,
Jessie died in August of the wounds she had received.

By the autumn the Dowager Empress and her court
had been driven from Peking by the Allied Armies of
Germany, Great Britain, Japan and Russia and the
Boxer Rising was virtually over. The punishments that
the Allies insisted should be meted out and the
reparations that were exacted accord ill with the
Saviour's command. 'Do good to those that hate you.'
Distinguishing between the respective claims of God

and Caesar is as difficult to Twentieth Century Christians as it was to those of the First.

PRAYER: *However dark the Way, Lord keep me in your Light.*

The Roman Catholic Church has beatified eighty-six of its Boxer martyrs, and the Russian Synodical Church outside of Russia honours several of the Orthodox Martyrs.

* * * * *

Sundar Singh   1889–1929

(*date unknown* in JUNE)

The Sikh religion, which as a boy Sundar imbibed deeply, is an attempt to combine the best of the religious tenets of both Islam and Hinduism. It differs chiefly from the latter by asserting that there is but one God, and from the former by a belief in reincarnation. For centuries it was a very peaceful religion emphasising the equality of all men before God and the importance of maternal love, but in the seventeenth century it took on a more warlike aspect as a result of persecutions. In this century many Sikhs have come to live in Britain and are easily recognised because some still wear turbans.

His mother died when he was fourteen and for Sundar it was a terrible blow. He had been her youngest son and she had long cherished the hope that he would become a Sadhu—a holy man. She herself had always practised her religion with intense devotion and done her best to foster a similar piety in her favourite boy.

'I was influenced,' he once wrote, 'more than the rest of the family by my mother's past life and teaching. She early impressed on me the rule that my first duty on rising in the morning was that I should pray to God for spiritual food and blessing, and that only after doing so I should break my fast. . . . Although at that time, I was too young to appreciate the value of those things, yet later on I realised their value, and now, whenever I think of it, I thank God for that training. I can never be sufficiently grateful to God for giving me such a mother, who in my earliest years instilled in me the love and fear of God.'

Not long before his mother's death Sundar had deliberately left a Christian Mission school that had been opened in his village, when he discovered that the New Testament was one of the books he would be expected to read. He was furious that, in the guise of the education which he wanted, an attempt had been made to compel him to study the Christian Scriptures. His mother's death not only drove him into a rebellion against his own religion but against God himself and when he was fifteen, in December 1903 he publicly burnt a copy of the Gospels.

'I thought that I had done a good deed,' he wrote much later, 'yet my unrest of heart increased and for the two following days I was very miserable. On the third day I could bear it no longer. I got up at three in the morning and prayed that if there was a God at all, he would reveal himself to me. My intention was that if I got no satisfaction, I would place my head upon the railway line when the five o'clock train passed by . . . I prayed and prayed but received no answer. At 4.30 . . . in the room where I was praying, I saw a great light. I thought the place was on fire. I looked around, but could find nothing . . . as I prayed and looked into the light, I saw the form of Jesus Christ . . . I heard a voice saying in Hindustani: "How long will you persecute me? I have come to save you; you were praying to know the right way. Why do you not take it?" So I fell at his feet and got this wonderful peace, which I could not get anywhere else . . . When I got up the vision had all disappeared but . . . the peace and joy have remained with me ever since.'

His family were horrified when he told them of his new found faith. First they ignored it, then they tried to argue him out of it. They refused to eat with him and at last begged him at least to keep his faith secret. He refused, was driven from his worldly home, and had to spend the first night under a tree.

He was baptised on his sixteenth birthday, 3 September 1905 in St Thomas's Church, Simla. When he left home he had eventually joined the Christian Boys' Boarding School at Ludhiana, but he was not a pupil for long and a month after his baptism his mother's prayers were answered and he declared himself to be a Christian Sadhu.

Once when asked about Christianity in India Sundar replied, 'The Water of Life has hitherto been offered to thirsting souls in India in a European vessel. Only when it is given in an Eastern bowl will it be accepted by simple men and women who seek the truth.' He had never taken to wearing European dress and was intensely proud of his Sikh ancestry. 'Christianity', he said, 'is the fulfilment of Hinduism. Hinduism has been digging channels. Christ is the water to flow through these channels. Hindus have received of the Holy Spirit. There are many beautiful things in Hinduism, but the fullest light is from Christ.' On another occasion he told the Archbishop of Upsala, 'So far as I can see, there are many more people among us in India who lead a spiritual life than there are in the West, although they do not know or confess Christ'.

For a while he became a member of a new Franciscan Community. It was his first meeting with the ideas of the Little Poor Man of Assisi, but Sundar like Francis himself, found it impossible to live his Christian life within particular structures. The Bishop of Lahore met the same response when he offered to ordain him. Sundar attended courses at a Theological college but would not accept ordination. As a Christian Sadhu he constantly journeyed through the Punjab, Kashmir, Baluchistan and even into Afghanistan, _ and in 1908 went to Tibet for the first time. His preaching was like our Lord's. He employed many parables taken from the everyday life and experience of his audience.

The Himalayas provided him with one theme. 'Till the sun's heat has melted the snow of the mountain tops it cannot flow down and irrigate the sun dried and musty plain. Until the snow is melted it cannot be drawn as water vapour to form clouds, from which it can come down as rain to make the parched and thirsty land green and fruitful. If we are not melted by the fire of the Holy Spirit we can neither quench the thirst of any famished soul nor bring him to the Fountain of Life where he will be satisfied and live for ever. May God give us grace so to live Christ in our daily lives, that we may be instrumental in bringing them to our Saviour.'

Sundar was instrumental, not only in India, but also in Europe, the Far East, America and Australasia in showing the whole world how, in the words of Archbishop Soderblom, 'the Gospel of Jesus Christ is reflected in unchanged purity in an Indian soul'. Above all he was a man of prayer, a mystic who spent long hours alone with his Lord.

In April 1929 he set off for another journey into Tibet. Physically he had not been well for five years, and his friends had noticed a certain sadness creeping into his face. In his passionate desire to follow Christ absolutely he had longed to die when he was thirty-four, the age at which Jesus is presumed to have been crucified, but he had not had his wish. Now he intended travelling to Tibet with some traders crossing the mountains through the Miti Pass. He had promised his friends to come back by the same route at about the end of June. Physically he was so unwell that they had tried to dissuade him but to no avail. They never saw him again. He must have died somewhere on the road into Tibet in May or June 1929.

PRAYER: *The life I now live is not my life, but the life which Christ lives in me (Gal 3.20).*

*   *   *   *   *

Florence Allshorn   1887–1950

(3 JULY)

In Uganda, fifty miles north of Lake Victoria at a place called Inganga, Florence Allshorn was crying her eyes out. It was 1920, she was then 33, and had been sent from England by the Church Missionary Society. When she arrived at the mission station she was put in charge of the girls' Boarding School. That part of life she enjoyed but there was a darker side. Seven young missionaries in as many years had been sent to that particular station but none had stayed. The problem was not only the climate, an exceedingly unhealthy one for Europeans, but the woman in charge. Nobody had been able to live with her for she had appalling fits of temper and at times was so moody that she wouldn't speak to her companion for days. When Florence arrived she had been shown into a sitting room in which at one end was arranged all the senior woman's furniture and the other end was entirely bare. That was her end.

She stuck it out for over a year, conscious that she was the eighth person who had been sent to work with and live alongside the older woman. No wonder she was weeping. Her own words must describe what followed. 'An old African matron came to me. She sat at my feet and after a time she said "I have been on this station for fifteen years and I have seen you come out, all of you, saying you have brought us a saviour, but I have never seen this situation saved yet." It brought me to my senses with a bang. I was the problem for myself. I knew enough of Jesus Christ to know that the enemy was the one to be loved before you could call yourself a follower of Jesus.' She began there and then what she later described as the little track everyone has to make in his life away from self to God. There was no miraculous healing of relationships but love was released and things improved so much that when Florence was about to leave she could say that Inganga had been the best home she had ever known.

It was in Sheffield that Florence had started active work within the Church, finding her base at the Cathedral which unlike older Cathedral foundations, also serves a parish. In 1918 she was appointed full time to the Cathedral staff and after two years, having offered herself to CMS was on a boat for Uganda.

When she left Inganga she expected to return to Africa after her break, but she became very ill with

Tuberculosis, which in those days meant almost certain death. An operation was suggested but she declined. Instead friends paid for her to go to a Sanatorium in Switzerland and she returned largely cured.

During her year's convalescence she stayed at Storrington in what today might be called a bohemian commune. All sorts of people were there; ex-convicts, down and outs, artists, Christians, atheists, agnostics, living in little huts or studios.

She hadn't been there long when an arrogant young man, Paul, hearing she was a missionary decided to shatter her illusions. Needless to say he failed. He also failed to shock her, instead they became firm friends and she was responsible for restoring some order into his own life.

She was like that, always wanting the best for people. Through all the bravado and cant she could see what kind of person Paul, might become. She once wrote 'I can't dislike people, I take Jesus Christ too seriously'. A friend said of her 'You could go to her room and at first be intensely aware of her, but after talking with her you would leave the room almost oblivious of her because you were so much more aware of God'.

In 1928 CMS asked Florence to take charge on a temporary basis of one of their training colleges for women missionaries, St Andrew's Hostel. It was an exciting challenge and Florence realised her experiences in Uganda were by no means unique. Young women with high ideals were in a few years completely broken in situations where only a cynic would say 'Look how these Christians love one another'. For ten years she remained as Principal, having seen the college through an amalgamation and other vissicitudes. She wanted herself and her students 'to be worthy to receive the terrible purity of God and also to be less difficult for other people to live with'. She never lost sight of the twofold commandment to love both God and our neighbours. She always asserted that the essentials at college were the student's life in God and capacity to live with her fellows.

As she left the college Florence was convinced that missionaries needed a second period of training after their first tour of duty, but there was nowhere for them to go. She set about filling the need. At the same time there was developing a further idea about community living and she and two companions early in 1940 began house hunting. They settled first in Haslemere at Easter 1941. There in an inconvenient house but amidst glorious surroundings Florence began the adventure which was to complete her life's work.

She and her companions had no intention to found a conventional Religious Community, living under the traditional vows of Poverty, Chastity and Obedience. Though the need to provide a place of refreshment, light and peace for missionaries on leave inspired them, they quickly became a refuge for many others, so quickly in fact that they soon outgrew their home in Haslemere and moved to a larger one at Barnes Green. It was there that the house and the community took the name St Julian's after an ancient Sussex saint noted for hospitality. In 1946 just after the last war they bought the neighbouring farm for use as a children's house, so that harrassed parents could come with their young families. The Community continued to grow and in 1950 moved finally to what was really a small estate of 460 acres with a large house, two farm houses, thirteen cottages, kitchen garden, lawn, terrace and a lake, complete with ducks.

By this time the household was organised on a regular basis. First was the community, who were responsible for the guest house and the farm, and who live together under a common rule of life. Alongside was a second more transient group who lived and worked with the community for short or long periods of as much as a year. Finally there were the guests themselves. Heading them all was Florence until she died on 3 July 1950.

As with her students, so with Community and guests, Florence always looked beyond their second best selves. At a talk not long before she died she said, 'To love a human being with the love of Christ means first of all to accept him as he is, and then to try to lead him towards a goal he doesn't see yet. Christ's love is entirely disinterested and selfless, it accepts you as you are, with all that is displeasing, disappointing and even painful for him in you, it gives love whatever the response may be; it forgives and forgives endlessly.'

PRAYER: *Jesus as you accept me as I am, may I accept others.*

* * * * *

Maria Theresa, Countess Ledochowska 1863–1922

(6 JULY)

When Countess Maria Theresa Ledochowska was asked what was necessary in order to join the community she had founded she replied, 'Courage, Humility and Generosity'. She knew what she was talking about, for those words exactly describe her own life. Maria Theresa was born in Austria on 29

April 1863, though her family were of Polish origin.
Her father was a retired soldier and they lived in a
large house at Loosdorf. Maria was a very precocious
child, writing a play to be performed by her family
when she was only five. At six she was keeping a diary
and had learned the Latin names of 300 plants and was
able to attach the right name to the right plant. Ten
years later after a trip to Poland with her father to visit
relations she published a travel book called *My Poland*.
Today a woman with such abilities would be able to
carve out for herself a useful and rewarding career, but
not so then. Living in the Imperial Palace at Salzburg,
the birthplace of the composer Mozart, were the
Grand Duke & Duchess of Tuscany who had lost their
Grand Duchy in Italy and retired to Austria in 1870 to
keep their court in Salzburg. Maria Theresa at 22 was
appointed Lady-in-Waiting to the Grand Duchess and
took up her duties in December 1885.

In some ways it must have been a very artificial life.
The Grand Duke and his Lady would have been
surrounded by all the pomp of an Imperial Court with
few of its responsibilities. Maria Theresa had always
been a devout Christian and while at court she continued to follow our Lord despite the thousand and
one distractions and temptations that would present
themselves in that glittering company.

And she continued to write. She was back to her five
year old love of plays and wrote many an interlude to
brighten the Imperial household. One day a friend
suggested she read the account of an address delivered in London by Cardinal Lavigerie concerning the
need for Christian work in Africa, especially in the
final drives to eradicate slavery throughout that conti-
nent. Hundreds of Catholic Christians used to go to
listen to the Cardinal and he inspired many to offer
themselves, their time, or their money for Missions in

Africa. In the course of this particular sermon he had said 'Let those who have a talent for writing place it at the service of this cause'. These words set Maria Theresa thinking.

Her first attempt to serve the cause was in a play *Zaida*. It was about African life and was read at court and actually produced in a Salzburg theatre. Soon all her spare time was occupied in getting as much information as possible into the hands of people who could help either directly by offering themselves for work in Africa or indirectly by providing for the needs of those who went out.

Maria Theresa could not both continue at court and carry on with her labours in support of Missionaries. Despite howls of protest from her family who called her 'Mission-Mad' she resigned her appointment in 1891 and began to write and circulate a little pamphlet about Catholic Mission work called *Echo from Africa*. Three years later she had been joined by one of her regular readers and a few other companions and by 1902 a new Religious congregation within the Roman Catholic Church, dedicated to the task of supporting the Missionary work of the Church in Africa had been officially recognised by the ecclesiastical authorities. Never in their wildest dreams had Maria Theresa's family seen her as a Foundress of a Religious Community. They would have wanted her to be married to a man from her own station in life and bring up a family. She travelled widely throughout Europe to talk to large numbers of Catholics about the needs of the Church in Africa; and in 1901 she earned a title that would have horrified her family. In jest someone called her, the 'Commercial Traveller of the African Missions'. By now *Echo from Africa*—mostly made up of excerpts of letters from Africa—was printed and published by her own Community in several European languages. Maria Theresa herself used to lecture in four languages. Thus she used her gift of language for the extension of God's Kingdom and provided opportunities for others to do the same. By the time of her death her community had sent out 197,570 books in nineteen different African languages for the use of the Church there.

Money was sent as well. One day a letter was received from a Bishop in Africa who wrote 'Constrained by the most urgent necessity and with entire confidence in your great kindness, I have allowed myself, almost in your name, to contract a debt of no less than 2000 rupees. I am sure that your heart, so sensible of the misfortunes of these poor unhappy Africans, could not bear to see them die of hunger.' Of course the Bishop had his money.

The last years of her life were spent in some physical suffering, but she remained a great influence for good within her congregation of sisters. She lived in her Community house in Rome and died there on 6 July 1922.

PRAYER: *Father I want courage to serve you and humility to take what comes.*

Maria Theresa Ledochowska was beatified by the Roman Catholic Church in 1975.

Maria Goretti   1890–1902

(6 JULY)

When Maria was eight Signor Goretti and his wife and family moved from the place where she, their third child, had been born to a village not far from Nettana on the Italian coast about forty miles from Rome.

The family, which included seven children in all, was quite poor and to save expense they even had to share a house. Two years after the move, Maria's father was dead and much of the domestic work had fallen on her young shoulders. She was an unusually religious and devout youngster, not only enjoying her church going, but prepared to walk miles in order to be present at Mass. Maria was also very beautiful and her beauty and innocence led to her destruction.

Signor Serenelli, with whom the Goretti family shared the house, had two sons, and the eldest, Alessandro, was naturally attracted to Maria. He tried to make love to her but she, young as she was, made it quite clear that she wanted nothing to do with him. Sometime in June 1902, when Maria was not yet twelve, he tried to assault her, but she managed to escape. However he warned her that if she were to tell anybody what had happened she would be killed. She knew he meant what he said.

A month later, 5 July 1902, Alessandro managed to ensure that he and Maria were alone in the house. He was armed with a dagger and threatened to kill her unless she allowed him to make love to her. In vain she pleaded with him, not for her own sake but his, for she wanted to prevent him committing a grave sin. In his passion Alessandro thrust a handkerchief in her mouth and pinioned her against the wall. His dagger was ready. He told her he would kill her unless she gave way. She would not. Savagely, Alessandro stabbed her fourteen times and left her bleeding to death on the stone floor. She was rushed to hospital and lived just long enough to forgive her murderer. The story does not end there. Alessandro as might be expected narrowly escaped being lynched. He was tried and sentenced to thirty years' imprisonment. He seemed entirely unrepentant for his crime, but by 1910, was a changed man. His genuine repentance was reflected in a dream he had of Maria coming to him and carrying a bunch of lilies, the universal symbol of purity.

PRAYER: *Lord, hold me back from sins of self-will, lest they get the better of me (Psalm 19.13).*

Maria Goretti was canonised by the Roman Catholic Church in 1950.

* * * * *

Ivan Vasilievich Moiseyev   1952–1972
(16 JULY)

The new recruits were shivering in gym kit on the parade ground of the USSR army barracks at Odessa. There was a gap in the ranks and from the other side of the ground a young soldier was desperately running to fill it. Breathlessly he took his place but the sergeant called out for an explanation of his late appearance. 'I am sorry, sir' gulped Ivan, as he tried to regain his breath. 'I was praying, sir.'

So began the trials of Ivan which were only to end

two years later in his martyrdom at Kerch on the Black Sea. His home was at Volontirovka in Moldavia, the second smallest of the constituent republics which make up Soviet Russia. All his immediate family apart from his elder brother were Christians, and when Ivan was called up for his two years' National Service his parents wondered what would happen to their handsome son who was never ashamed to confess the faith of Christ crucified.

Although the constitution of the USSR grants freedom of religion to all its citizens, in practice the state is determinedly atheist and the military authorities had no intention of allowing a young Christian to propagate his belief among the ranks. The trouble in Ivan's case was that he was a good soldier who, in six months, earned seven recommendations from his officers. He was liked by his comrades and his response to constant interrogations or the cruelties inflicted on him was to seize every opportunity of talking about God and his only son Jesus Christ. The men too began to wonder how it was that Ivan survived being made to stand outside their hut every night for a fortnight clad only in summer uniform when the temperature was 13° below freezing point.

One evening in barracks the men were waiting for a lecture. The lecturer hadn't turned up and the discussion turned to religion. When Vanya—that was the name his family and friends used—claimed that God was omnipotent, one of the sergeants challenged him to prove it. 'If your God can do anything, let him get me leave tomorrow to go home. Then I'll believe in him.' The sergeant got his leave. On another occasion when Vanya was in hospital after he had been involved in an accident under a lorry, he heard the doctors talking about the surgery that was necessary. They were going to amputate his arm. He prayed earnestly and next morning when the surgeons were around his bed they found him cured. One can imagine the fury of his commanding officer who had tried his level best to knock faith out of the young man, when he heard on the other end of the telephone a surgeon telling him that there had been a miracle. 'There really is a God.'

Six months or so later the CO found himself in the presence of Vanya's parents come to collect the body of their son, who, so the official report went, had drowned in the Black Sea. 'I was present when your son died,' he told them. 'He fought with death, he died hard, but he died a Christian.' He was speaking the truth. Vanya had died by drowning, but only after he had all but perished under torture. When his parents opened his coffin they found the tell-tale marks of his suffering on his body. In an open letter to all Christians they declared 'Knowing Vanya to be a faithful witness of Christ, we declare he was tormented and tortured for Jesus'.

PRAYER: *Jesus I don't want to boast of anything except your cross (Gal 6.14).*

* * * * *

Andrew Kaguru   c 1909–1953

(25 JULY)

To the north and west of Nairobi, the capital city of Kenya, there lived and still lives a tribe of people called Kikuyu. In earlier days the Kikuyu were warriors, though never particularly savage or brave, but now they have mostly become farmers, keeping cattle and goats and living in traditional style mud huts.

A European Christian first visited the tribe at the beginning of the twentieth century. He made his headquarters at the small town of Fort Hall and from there set off for the Kikuyu homelands in the Aberdare mountains. The Kikuyu were not very anxious to listen to him for they feared their ancestors would be angry if they worshipped the Christian God. They were scared too of their High God Ngai, who lived as they thought, in Mount Kenya, the highest peak of the Aberdares. The missionary was not discouraged. He opened a school in a place called Kiruri and one of his first pupils was a very quarrelsome boy Kaguru who was always fighting, especially with boys younger or smaller than himself.

Kaguru proved to be a reasonable scholar and was sent to another school at a nearby town, Wathagu, but he only stayed there for a few months because he was bitten by jiggers, little insects that burrow themselves under the skin. He returned home, but in 1922, he and his family moved to Fort Hall. There they all worked for a white man, Frank Watkins, called Gateru, 'Man with a beard,' by the natives.

Nearly all the farms in that area were owned by white men. They employed a great number of the Africans and these lived in their own huts on the farmer's land. Each native had his own plot of land which he could farm and at least two huts. The huts were surrounded by a fence and the whole was called a Shamba. Kaguru lived with his mother and sister in a Shamba and he began working as turkey boy, looking after a large flock of turkeys for Gaturu's wife. He did his job well and was soon the general handyman of the farm.

He had not been long on the farm when a school-church was built by the Africans. Gaturu gave them wood and the other materials, and the men helped in the building after they had finished their work on the farm. Kaguru helped and when the school was opened he joined a class so that he could continue his studies. He also began to go to church on Sundays, and eventually asked for baptism and was received into the Church by the name of Andrew.

In 1938, Andrew Kaguru married a girl called Alice. Although her parents were not Christians Alice was baptised, but she didn't see much point in being a Christian for it seemed to make little difference to Andrew who was as quarrelsome as ever and often drunk.

Soon after their marriage Gaturu died and Andrew and Alice went with Mrs Hill, Gaturu's daughter, to a farm she had bought at Sabukia. They had not been settled for long when their employer was taken very ill and had to go to hospital; Andrew was left in charge of the farm. Mrs Hill was a bit worried by what some of her friends said when they visited her in hospital. 'You'll find they've pinched all your things,' they assured her. 'You ought to have got a European to take charge.' She need not have worried. Every week Andrew bicycled to the hospital to tell her about the farm and when she was well enough to go home, she found everything in order. Andrew was gradually becoming a different kind of man.

Alice had noticed the change in her husband. The religion that she thought meant very little to him, now seemed much more important. There were few priests in Kenya and many churches could only have a service if there was a lay-man to take them. It was during a sermon by a visiting preacher that Andrew came to understand more clearly that God is holy, that He knows even the thoughts of our hearts and that He hates the sin that He sees there. When Mrs Hill sold the farm she offered to help Andrew find another job. He refused. He had made up his mind to return home to help to lead his fellow Kikuyu tribesmen to serve the Lord.

At Kiruri, apart from helping with services, Andrew taught in the school and visited folk in their homes. Many of them had been baptised, often when at school, but it had made very little difference to them, as it had once made little difference to Andrew. He made it his special task to search out these men and women and encourage them to return to Our Lord's service and for five years he worked as a diligent and faithful pastor.

When the British began to govern Kenya, one of the first things they did, often through the Churches, was to start schools. Some of the students were soon ready for higher education and often came to universities in Britain. On their return to Kenya they wanted, quite rightly, to be able to join in the government of their land, but in 1952, Kenya was still a British Colony. Some of them were impatient for the time when power would be handed over and they began to organise among the Kikuyu a terrible secret society called Mau Mau. To join the Society, a man, and sometimes even a woman, had to take an oath, administered by a special witch-doctor, which usually involved human sacrifice. By it they promised to support the Mau Mau in murders, and attacks on white farms. Sometimes the victim for the sacrifice was a white man, but often it was an African, a Kikuyu who refused to take the oath. One Mau Mau warning, nailed to a tree included the sentence 'Anyone refusing to take the Mau Mau oath or does not take steps to try and take it, he is not a true African and must die'.

Most natives who refused to be bound by the oath, did so because they were Christians not because they wanted the British to continue to rule their country. It was essential to the leaders' plans, however, that as few Kikuyu as possible should avoid becoming members and therefore they organised a campaign of terror. Many took the oath, often after seeing one of their number tortured, beheaded or hacked to pieces by the gang. Christian pastors and leaders did their best to encourage their flocks to remain steadfast, and Andrew was particularly outspoken. Unfortunately some of his congregation had taken the oath and they reported to their Mau Mau leaders what Andrew had said.

A few nights later, after midnight, when Andrew and his family were all sound asleep, some of the gang, armed with spears and knives, crept from the mountains and stole towards the hut. They battered down the door and seized both Andrew and Alice. Andrew was hit by one of the men who stood over him holding an evil looking spear. Two others held Alice and forced her to look towards her husband.

'Will you take the oath, or we will kill your husband?' growled the leader.

'Never,' she cried. 'I am a Christian.'

'We will save you, if you will.'

'We will never do it,' said Andrew, 'So what you are going to do, do quickly.'

One of the men struck Alice, and then they beat her, cut her neck, arm and leg and threw her violently on to the floor. She hit her head and became unconscious.

The noise, and their mother's cries had awoken the children. Terrified, the eldest pulled open the door that led to their parents' room, but he was pushed back roughly by one of the gang. Meanwhile Andrew had been dragged outside the hut and there cut to death.

In 1955, the then Archbishop of Canterbury, Dr Geoffrey Fisher, laid the foundation stone of the new Cathedral at Fort Hall. It is dedicated to St James and All Martyrs, and is the church built in honour of Andrew and the many other Kenya Christians, possibly more than fifteen hundred, who gave their lives for their Faith. During his sermon the Archbishop said, 'It is very, very, humbly that I speak to you, only praying, that if such a decision ever came to me, I might be as faithful as some of you have been'.

PRAYER: *The Lord is my light and my salvation; whom should I fear (Psalm 27.1).*

The names of over a hundred Kikuyu Martyrs appear in the Book of Anglican Modern Martyrs in St Paul's Cathedral, London.

* * * * *

Edith Stein   1891–1942
(9 AUGUST)

Edith was brought up at Breslau in Germany in a devout Jewish home. Her father had died when she was very young, but every Sabbath she had gone with her mother to the synagogue. She had watched her mother prepare the family's food in strict accordance with the Jewish law and of course she had learned Hebrew. She suffered as a Jewess even when a school girl, for although she had a brilliant mind she never came first in class because her teacher detested the Jewish people. At twenty she began to study German language and literature, history, philosophy and experimental psychology in the University at Breslau. She continued with some of these studies at Göttingen.

Although she had attended synagogue when she was at Breslau University so as not to hurt her mother, Edith had at thirteen become an atheist. At Göttingen she met another Jewish family Adolph and Anna Reinach. Adolph was also a teacher of philosophy but he and his wife were on the verge of becoming Christians. He was called up for service in the German Army in 1914, and in 1916 Adolph and Anna were baptised. A year later Adolph was dead, killed in Flanders, and his wife begged Edith to sort out, presumably for publication, various papers concerning his work. Edith agreed but was miserable at the thought of going to that home to find, not the happy couple she had known but 'the sombre shadows of deep mourning'. She found nothing of the sort. She discovered Anna Reinach radiant in her unshakeable faith in a living God. Edith was to say later that that that been her first encounter with the cross and the divine strength it inspires in those who carry it. 'At that moment my unbelief was utterly crushed . . . and the light of Christ poured into my heart—the light of Christ in the mystery of the Cross.'

She still delayed asking for Baptism. Her heart was convinced but her mind still needed to be satisfied. That finally happened on holiday when, one evening alone on a farm of a friend she picked up the autobiography of St Teresa of Avila, the great Spanish reformer of the Carmelite Order of Nuns. The book enthralled Edith. She read it through all that night and by morning knew she had found *Truth*. She was baptized in the early morning of New Year's Day, 1922 in the parish church of Bergzabern and in some ways would have liked to have joined the Carmelites immediately but there were many reasons why she should not. First she had to tell her mother, and she knew how much grief her conversion would cause. To make it easier for the old lady, Edith stayed with her for several months, going with her to synagogue as well as attending Mass at the local church. Eventually she had to return to work and was given the post of a teacher at a Dominican Convent School in Speyer. The Nuns allowed her to live within the convent itself and there she quickly learned to love the regular daily round of services in their Chapel. Her life was very simple and she spent hours in prayer, but still she remained unsatisfied.

Edith remained at Speyer for eight years, until she was asked to undertake lecturing to adults, particularly women through the Institute of Education at Munster. On 30 January 1933 Hitler became Chancellor of Germany. By the following October Edith had left her work at the Institute, said goodbye to the mother who loved her so much but could not understand what her favourite daughter was doing, and entered the enclosure of the Carmelites in Cologne to begin a new life of dedication to God.

During those last weeks with her mother Edith had reminded her that before a woman was allowed to take the solemn life vows of a nun, she had first to live with her new Christian family for a time as a novice and that during that time she might leave whenever she wished. Her mother was not to be so easily comforted. 'If *you* undertake a time of trial' she said, 'I know you will go through with it.' Frau Stein knew her daughter.

Edith, now called Sister Benedicta, remained in

Cologne until 31 December 1938, when for her own safety and the wellbeing of the convent, she was sent to a Carmelite priory at Acht in Holland. During her years in Germany she had completed a theological treatise and was seeing it through the press. It was not to be published until after the last war, for no publisher in Nazi Germany dare print anything by a Jew. She was finally told this in Holland, but even there she was able to go on with her studies. But it is not for her intellect that she is best remembered. She wrote hundreds of letters to all kinds of people, encouraging and leading them in the Christian way. She spent hours in prayer and did her best to share in the sufferings of her people throughout Europe. By now her sister Rosa who had also become a Christian, was in Holland as well, living near the convent and for a time the two met every day so that Edith was fully aware of what was happening.

In July 1941 she learned that one of her brothers and his family had been taken to a concentration camp. She knew that it would not be long before she too had to suffer, but she was ready, anxious to offer her life and so help to complete 'the full tale of Christ's afflictions' (Col 1.24).

Meanwhile the nuns were trying to get both Edith and Rosa to Switzerland—and safety. Passports were applied for. Edith and her sister were summoned to Gestapo Headquarters. As she entered, instead of raising her hand in salute and shouting as was expected of her 'Heil Hitler' this intrepid woman cried, 'Praise to Jesus Christ'. It was hardly appreciated by the Germans. She was insulted and sent back to her convent with a yellow star which all Jews had to stitch on their clothes.

On 11 July every Christian Church in Holland sent telegrams to the Nazi authorities protesting at the

persecution of the Jews. They carried their protests
still further and as a reprisal all Jews were to be
arrested. Sister Benedicta and Rosa were bundled into
police vans and sent to a local concentration camp at
Westerbook. A Jewish businessman who managed to
survive has written this account of their arrival:

'Among the prisoners who arrived on 5 August,
Sister Benedicta made a striking impression by her
great calm and composure. The misery in the camp
and the excitement among the newcomers were
indescribable. Sister Benedicta walked about among
the women, comforting, helping, soothing like an
angel. Many mothers were almost demented and
had for days not been looking after their children,
but had been sitting brooding in listless despair.
Sister Benedicta at once took care of the poor little
ones, washed and combed them, and saw to it that
they got food and attention.'

She was not in that camp long. On 7 August she was
pushed in a train destined for Auschwitz. On the 9th
she and her sister became two of the 4,000,000 people,
largely Jews, who perished in the gas chambers there.
'To be a child of God' she once wrote 'means to place
every care and every hope in the Hand of God and not
to worry about oneself or one's future.'

PRAYER: *May Jesus Christ be praised for ever and ever.*

Sister Benedicta is to be beatified by her church.

Maximilian Kolbe   1894–1941

(14 AUGUST)

His mother was cross with him and had made her
displeasure felt in a good hiding. In exasperation she
cried out to her ten-year-old scapegrace 'What ever is
going to become of you when you grow up?' Few
children would have taken much notice of that but
Raymond was an exception. He worried over it for the
rest of that day and was still worrying when he said his
prayers before climbing into his bed. That night he had
a dream. He saw our Lord's Mother—along with
millions of Christians Raymond called her 'Our
Lady'—holding two crowns in her hand, one white
and the other red. She asked him if he were willing to
accept either of them. The white one meant that when
he grew up he would give up the possibility of a wife
and family and join a religious order, and the red one
meant he would die for Our Lord. In his dream he
chose both crowns and from that time his life changed
radically. He now knew what would become of him.

He began to train for the priesthood and it was soon
clear to his teachers that he was a young man of great
potential. In 1910 he became a Franciscan taking the
name of Maximilian. Even before he was ordained at
Rome in 1918, with six companions he had founded a
missionary crusade which he naturally dedicated to
our Lady. For a while in his late teens he had toyed
with the idea of becoming a soldier, and now as a
priest he wanted to battle against the enemies of Christ
in his native Poland.

Although only twenty-five he was a sick man in an
advance stage of tuberculosis, but he threw himself
into missionary activity forming small groups of devout Christians all over Poland. In 1922 he began to

publish a monthly magazine to show the way to true happiness. By 1927 70,000 copies were being printed each month, and their premises were obviously too small. Maximilian, as we must now call him, began to look for something larger and nearer to Warsaw. He was offered land at Teresin, West of the capital, and in November 1927 his big family of Friars moved in. Yet again it was dedicated to Mary and given the Polish title 'Niepokalanow'. At first it consisted of no more than a few shacks with tar-paper roofs, but it flourished, and before long had become one of the largest Franciscan houses in the world. In 1930 Maximilian with four brothers left Poland to begin similar work in Japan. They did so successfully but in 1936 Maximilian was recalled home by his superiors.

By 13 September 1939 Niepokalanow had been occupied by the invading Germans and most of its inhabitants had been deported to Germany. Among them was Maximilian, but not long afterwards they were inexplicably set free. From the moment of his return to Niepokalanow, Maximilian was organising shelter for 3,000 Polish refugees, among whom were 2,000 Jews, the friars sharing everything they had with their guests.

Inevitably the community came under suspicion and was closely watched. Early in 1941, in the only edition of their magazine which was allowed to be published Maximilian wrote 'No one in the world can change Truth. What we can do and should do is to seek truth and to serve it when we have found it. The real conflict is an inner conflict. Beyond armies of occupation and the hecatombs of extermination camps, there are two irreconcilable enemies in the depth of every soul; good and evil, sin and love. And what use are the victories on the battlefield if we ourselves are defeated in our innermost selves?' After that plain speaking he was arrested and sent to the infamous Pawiak prison in Warsaw. Here he was singled out for special ill-treatment. An SS guard, seeing him in his habit asked if he believed in Christ. When Maximilian replied, 'I do' the guard struck him. The question was repeated several times receiving always the same answer. The beating continued mercilessly. Shortly afterwards the Franciscan habit was taken away and he was compelled to wear a prisoner's uniform.

On 28 May Maximilian with over 300 others was deported to the concentration camp in Auschwitz. There he was branded with the number 16670. He was put to work immediately with other priests carrying blocks of stone for the construction of a crematorium wall. He was assigned to the Babice section under the direction of 'Bloody' Krott, an ex-criminal, who forced the prisoners to cut and carry huge tree-trunks. The work went on all day without a break and had to be done at the double, encouraged by vicious blows from the guards. Once Krott found some of the heaviest planks he could lay hold of and personally loaded them on the Franciscan's back. He ordered Maximilian to run and when he collapsed, Krott kicked him in the stomach and face, and had his men give him fifty lashes. He lost consciousness and Krott threw him in the mud for dead, but his companions managed to smuggle him to the camp hospital.

In Auschwitz, where hunger and hatred reigned and faith evaporated Maximilian opened his heart to others and spoke of God's infinite love. He never seemed to think of himself. When food was brought in and everyone struggled to get a place in the queue to be sure of his share Maximilian stood aside, so that frequently there was none left for him. At other times he shared his meagre ration of soup or bread with others. He once told another priest 'We must be grateful we are here. There is so much for us to do. Look how people need us.'

In July 1941, a prisoner escaped from Block 14. The commandant's deterrent after an escape was to confine 20 prisoners in a starvation cell from which they never emerged alive. The morning after the prisoner's disappearance, the commandant ordered all inmates of the block to the parade ground. They stood there in the sun all day. In the evening the commandant said that for the last time he would be merciful. Only 10, not 20 would be put in the cell.

He began to choose his victims. Three had been selected and his finger was pointing to the fourth, Francicek Gajowinczek, a Polish army sergeant, who broke down crying for mercy, 'I have a wife and two children. I want to see them again. I don't want to die.' Maximilian left the ranks, hurried towards the commandant and tried to kiss his hand. The commandant pushed him away. 'What does this Polish pig want?' he asked the interpreter. Maximilian said he wished to take the sergeant's place. The soldier went back to his place, and Maximilian and the nine others were marched away.

Daily from the airless underground cell rose the loud prayers of the condemned men led by Maximilian. They were often so deep in prayer that they did not hear inspecting SS men descend to the Bunker. Their voices fell silent only at the loud yelling of their visitors. When the cells were opened the poor wretches cried loudly and begged for a piece of bread and for water. If any of the stronger ones approached the door he was immediately kicked in the stomach by the SS men, so that falling backwards on the cement floor he might be killed or else he was shot. Maximilian bore up bravely, he did not beg nor did he complain, but raised the spirits of the others, and as they grew weaker and weaker, their prayers became faint whispers. At every inspection, when almost all the others were lying on the floor, Maximilian was found kneeling or standing in the centre to look cheerfully in the face of the SS men. Two weeks passed. One after another the men died, until only Maximilian was left. It was too long; the cell was needed for new victims. They brought in the head of the sick-quarters, to give Maximilian an injection of carbolic acid.

PRAYER: *Thank you for letting me serve you anywhere.*

Maximilian Kolbe was beatified by the Roman Catholic Church in 1971, and later canonised by his fellow Pole, Pope John Paul II.

*   *   *   *   *

John Leonard Wilson   1897–1970

(18 AUGUST)

Leonard Wilson's life was by no means smooth and easy. He was very unhappy at school; found the theology of some of his fellow Anglicans narrow and hard to stomach in his early years as a priest, and throughout his life was unable to cope happily in debate with Christians whose views differed fundamentally from his own. Indeed his biographer suggests that he was in essence an autocrat and hopeless as a chairman in meetings where ideas diametrically opposed to his were raised. Yet it is his name that is incised on the floor of the chancel in Birmingham

Cathedral bearing beneath it the legend 'Confessor for the Faith'.

It had not always been so. Leonard never found faith an easy thing, and was frankly agnostic about certain statements in the Creeds, but his experiences at the hands of the Japanese confirmed his trust in God and completely justify his epitaph.

When the Japanese invaded Singapore in World War Two, Leonard was bishop of the diocese. The colony surrendered in February 1942 and for over a year Leonard and many others were allowed compara- tive freedom to carry on their work. This was partly due to the fact that one of the Japanese officers with civil authority in the colony was himself a Christian and used regularly to attend services in the Cathedral. All this changed in March 1943 when the European civilians were interned in Changi Prison. Seven months later the Japanese Military Police took over control of the prison and it was subsequently dis- covered that they had done so because they had been convinced that there was a spy organisation in Changi Prison which received and transmitted messages by radio telephone. They also belived that the organisa- tion was responsible for stirring up anti-Japanese feeling in the town to encourage acts of sabotage, and that it collected money for this purpose. As it hap- pened none of these accusations were true, but Leonard as a leader of the Christians was taken with other prominent citizens to the Police HQ in 17 October 1943.

For three days he was subjected to the most brutal tortures so that he almost prayed for death. This is how he later spoke about it on radio. 'In the middle of that torture they asked me if I still believed in God, when by God's help, I said "I do", they asked my why God did not save me, and by the help of his Holy

Spirit, I said "God does save me. He does not save me by freeing me from pain or punishment but he saves me by giving me the spirit to bear it." And when they asked me why I did not curse them, I told them that it was because I was a follower of Jesus Christ, who taught us that we were all brethren. I did not like to use the words, "Father, forgive them". It seemed too blasphemous to use our Lord's words, but I felt them, and I said, "Father I know these men are doing their duty. Help them to see I am innocent." And when I muttered, "Forgive them," I wondered how far I was being dramatic and if I really meant it, because I looked at their faces as they stood around and took it in turns to flog, and their faces were hard and cruel and some of them were evidently enjoying their cruelty. But by the grace of God I saw those men not as they were, but as they had been. Once they were little children playing with their brothers and sisters and happy in their parents' love, in those far-off days before they had been conditioned by their false nationalist ideals, and it is hard to hate little children, but even that was not enough. There came into my mind, as I lay there, the words of that Communion hymn:

> Look Father, look on his anointed face,
>   And only look on us as found in him;
> Look not on our misusings of thy grace,
> Our prayer so languid, and our faith so dim;
>   For lo! between our sins and their reward
> We set the Passion of Thy Son our Lord.

And so I saw them, not as they were, not as they had been, but as they were capable of becoming, redeemed by the power of Christ, and I knew it was only common sense to say "Forgive".'

Four years later, the War over, Leonard was conducting a Confirmation in his cathedral. At least one of those who knelt before him was Japanese, Leonard couldn't help recognizing him. He had been one of his torturers.

When he returned to England, Leonard was appointed first Dean of Manchester Cathedral and then Bishop of Birmingham. He retired at the end of September 1969 and died a year later.

PRAYER: *Jesus, more and more yourself display, shining to the perfect day.*

*   *   *   *   *

Giuseppe Melchiore Sarto (Pope Pius X)   1835–1914

(21 AUGUST)

Many, many people who met Giuseppe when he was Pope were conscious of his goodness. As the spiritual head of Roman Catholic Christians he is regarded by some of his co-religionists as being a far too rigid defender of the Church's civil rights; and by others as the man who purged the church of modern erroneous thinking, but none would deny his deep love of God and his intense care for all men. It is often said of him that he died of a broken heart when efforts to avert the First World War failed.

He was an Italian born into a very poor family in the little village of Riese near Venice on 2 June 1835. Giuseppe's father was the village postman and Giuseppe was the second child in the family of ten. He first went to the local school and from thence, through the encouragement of his parish priest, to the gram-

mar school at Castelfranco, walking five miles there
and back every day. He decided to be a priest quite
early in his life and after his ordination in 1857 devoted
himself for seventeen years to parish work. By 1884 he
had been consecrated Bishop of Mantua, a diocese
that was then in very poor shape. So well did he
manage the affairs of the Church there that in 1892 he
was made Patriarch of Venice. Eleven years later Pope
Leo XIII died and Giuseppe, by now a Cardinal, was
summoned to Rome with the rest of the sacred college
to elect Leo's successor. Not for a moment did he
imagine that he would be the choice; he had a return
ticket for Venice in his pocket.

During his Papacy he tried to establish some sort of
agreement between the Church and the State in his
own country, and in that he was largely successful.
Opinion differs about his handling of Church/State
relations in France but at least he managed to put a
stop to the French Government having any veto over
the appointment of Bishops.

In his first encyclical—that is a letter to all Christians—he had said that he wanted to see all things
renewed in Christ and nothing was better calculated to
do that than his instructions concerning the Eucharist.
He recommended daily communion when possible,
directed that children in the Roman Catholic Church
should be allowed to receive Holy Communion at an
early age, and made the communion of the sick much
easier. He also strongly urged daily reading of the
Bible—but here with a few exceptions his words fell
on deaf ears.

Guiseppe, or Pius X as he was now called, was
always concerned for the weak and oppressed. He
was especially strong in his denunication of the foul
treatment of the Indians on the rubber plantations of
Peru and greatly encouraged missions there. He sent

relief after an earthquake at Messina and sheltered refugees at his own expense in a hospice by St Peter's in Rome. His general charities throughout the world were so great that people wondered where all the money came from, while his simplicity and goodness shone out as he preached in one of the Vatican courtyards every Sunday. He was embarrassed, perhaps a little shocked, by the ceremonies of the papal court. At Venice he had refused to let anyone but his sisters cook for him, and now he refused to carry out the custom of conferring titles on them. 'The Lord has made them sisters of the pope,' he said, 'That should suffice'. 'Look how they have dressed me up', he exclaimed once to an old friend, and burst into tears. To another he said ruefully 'They lead me about surrounded by soldiers like Jesus when he was seized in Gethsemane'. He was later to write in his Will 'I was born poor and I wish to die poor too'.

He, along with many others, had foreseen the outbreak of the First World War. When it was declared on the anniversary of his election to the Papacy he wrote:

'This is the last affliction that the Lord will visit on me. I would gladly give my life to save my poor children from this ghastly scourge.'

Soon afterwards the Austrian Ambassador appeared before him and announced rather grandly,

'Holy Father, thousands of Catholics march in the armies of Austria and Germany. His Majesty the Emperor of Austria has asked you to bless his armies in the struggle.'

Pius X was speechless for a moment and then replied,

'I bless peace not war'.

The Ambassador left, deflated.

After a few days' illness, Pius developed bronchitis and died on 20 August 1914.

PRAYER: *Lord give strength to your people: Lord bless your people with peace (Psalm 29.11).*

Pope Pius X was canonised by his Church in 1954.

*   *   *   *   *

Simone Weil   1900–1943

(24 AUGUST)

'I cannot help still wondering in these days when so large a proportion of humanity is sunk in materialism, if God does not want there to be some men and women who have given themselves to him and to Christ and who yet remain outside the church.' Simone wrote that in a letter to a Father Perrin of Marseilles in 1942. She had been introduced to him soon after she and her family fled to Vichy France from Paris and German occupied territory. Although no longer believers, they were Jews by birth and therefore in great danger, but luckily they were able to get a boat to the United States. From America Simone went on to London to join the Free French and died in a Kent Sanatorium in August 1943. Her letters to Father Perrin were a final attempt on her part to explain to him why she would not ask for Baptism.

Simone had been something of a rebel all her life. During the First World War she had part of her rations sent to the soldiers at the front, and refused to eat sugar because they had to go without it too. In winter she refused to wear stockings so that she could share the lot of the ragged urchins of Paris, though perhaps she was more concerned to make her parents uncomfortable with their own high standard of living amidst so much poverty.

After a brilliant academic career she taught philosophy in a number of schools and very soon began to take an active part in politics. Her revolutionary and extreme left wing views brought her into constant conflict with the educational authorities, but she never actually joined the communist or socialist parties, contenting herself with defending the weak and oppressed, irrespective of race or party. Wishing to share to the uttermost the lot of the poor she took a year's leave from teaching and worked in a car factory without letting anyone know who she was. She rented a room in the workmen's area and lived entirely on her very small wages. The incredible monotony of the work convinced her that there was little hope of a real social revolution emanating from the factory floor.

During the Spanish Civil War Simone fought on the side of the Reds, but was of little help to them. She never fired a gun, and once when cooking for her unit managed to scald herself so badly with boiling oil she had to go to hospital, until her parents fetched her home to Paris. She returned to teaching in 1937 and, on holiday in that year, visited Assisi. There, alone in the little twelfth-century Romanesque chapel of St Mary of the Angels, where once St Francis had heard the Lord say, 'Francis re-build my church' something compelled Simone for the first time in her life to go down on her knees. The following year she spent Holy

Week and Easter at the Benedictine Monastery of Solesme, famous throughout the world for its plain-song. She had been very ill and still suffered appalling migraines but she followed the Liturgy carefully and in her own words 'The thought of the Passion of Christ entered into my being once and for all.'

An English guest at the Monastery introduced her to the poems of George Herbert, a seventeenth-century Anglican priest. His poem *Love* fascinated her. The first two lines 'Love bade me welcome; yet my soul drew back, guilty of dust and sin' summed up how she felt. She learned the whole poem off by heart and used to recite it to herself over and over again. 'I used to think,' she wrote in her letter to Father Perrin, 'I was merely reciting it as a beautiful poem, but without my knowing it the recitation had the virtue of prayer. It was during one of these recitations that Christ himself came down and took possession of me . . . I felt in the midst of my suffering the presence of a love, like that which one can read in the smile on a beloved face.'

When she and her family had moved south, Simone made friends with a farmer, Gustave Thibon. He was a Christian and she had a great effect on him. Like Father Perrin he longed for her to become a member of the Church. After all she believed in Christ, spent long hours in prayer, passionately believed in the sacramental presence of Christ in the Eucharist, and attended Mass regularly. She would not seek baptism. 'It is not my business to think about myself,' she said, 'My business is to think about God. It is for God to think about me.' She began studying the New Testament in Greek and after she had come to the story of Jesus giving his disciples the 'Our Father' she used to repeat the prayer in the original Greek every day. If, as she was saying it, her attention wandered, she would go back to the beginning and start afresh, and would do so over and over again until she had gone through it once with full attention.

When she arrived in England she was given the task by the French Government in exile of writing a report on the possibilities of building up a new and more just social structure in France after the war. Although in the comparative safety of England, she wanted to share the sufferings of her fellow countrymen in occupied France, so she refused to eat more than the lowest rations there and thus by starvation hastened her death from tuberculosis.

PRAYER: *Lord it's not my business to worry about myself—I can leave that to You.*

* * * * *

Vivian Frederick Barnes
Redlich   1905–1942
and the New Guinea martyrs

(2 SEPTEMBER)

One day early in 1935, or perhaps late in 1934, a young bespectacled clergyman with long neck, and ears that were a trifle large was sitting in the London office of the secretary of a Missionary Society when another clergyman came into the room. He was the representative in England of the Anglican Bishop of Rockhampton in Australia, and asked 'Can you find me a man for the Bush Brotherhood in Rockhampton?'

'Yes' replied the secretary pointing to the young

clergyman with glasses, 'There he sits'. Vivian could not find a suitable answer and on 27 April 1935 he sailed for Australia. Since he was fifteen his home had been in the small Leicestershire village of Little Bowden where his father was the Rector, though after his own ordination at Wakefield in May 1932 he had been curate of St John's, Dewsbury Moor. It was at Dewsbury that Vivian heard first hand accounts of the work of a Bush Brother when the Bishop of Rockhampton came to talk to a Missionary School which Vivian had organised for the parish.

Vivian seems to have enjoyed his curacy, being best remembered for his work among children and the Scouts, and he had an influence on boys and young men that was to last all their lives. His Vicar must have found him trying at times and understandably thought him a little immature for he was much given to practical jokes and anyone might be his victim, even the Bishop of the Diocese when he paid a visit to Vivian's Rover Crew.

Bush Brotherhoods in Australia were quasi-religious communities within the Anglican Church there. The Brother gave himself to the Brotherhood for a set number of years and during that time he would take his full share in ministering to the small groups, mainly of settlers from Britain, who lived widely separated over immense areas in the Northern half of Australia.

Vivian joined the Bush Brotherhood of St Andrew which was attached to the Rockhampton Diocese, Central Queensland, and his headquarters were at Winton at a little wooden church of St Paul. The Brothers' parish however was about the area of England. Vivian had one colleague who looked after all the towns in their enormous parish while Vivian coped with the scattered communities around, and that could mean for him round trips of over sixteen hundred miles.

In 1940 Vivian offered himself for work on New Guinea and a year later after he had had experience helping in another station, the Bishop of New Guinea asked him to take charge of the station at Sangara, about fifty miles from Port Moresby on the South coast of the island. The responsibility obviously delighted him and when he arrived, there was a great deal to do. To start with Vivian found a hundred and forty Catachumens ready for Baptism and after he had made a font out of beaten copper, he began to baptize them at intervals in groups of twenty.

Making a font was almost part of an ordinary day's work. Vivian was a typical handyman. In Theological College at Chichester he had driven an old Morris Cowley which was held together almost by string. At Dewsbury Moor he had wired up the Rover Den for electricity, and his exploits with 'Evangeline' the mission car in Queensland were hilarious. At Sangara he was soon building a cottage hospital, and his own generator to provide lighting and power, making spare parts from scrap and old tin cans. In April 1942 he was thinking in terms of more pioneer work, opening up another station further inland if only he could be sent a teacher for it.

When his Bishop visited him in June of that year he found Vivian so unwell that he took him back with him to the Diocesan Headquarters at Dogura. War had broken out and the Japanese threat to New Guinea was a very real one, so Vivian was reluctant to leave his people. His Bishop insisted but Vivian promised that he would return as soon as he was fit. A Government doctor, a Roman Catholic, continues the story of what happened after that.

'Saturday 25 July 1942, is a day I shall not easily

forget. Early that day I had escaped from the Japanese, mainly through the help of one of the Sangara mission boys. Much to my surprise, I learned from the natives that Fr Redlich was again in the district and in hiding quite close to the mission house. About six o'clock in the evening, with a few natives, I left one of the villages to get in touch with him. Just on dusk I reached his shelter. The village people had built him a lean-to on the side of a hill, and had posted watchers along the track.

'From Fr Vivian I learnt that he had arrived at Oro Bay in the mission boat as the Japanese were shelling Buna. By working hard, he landed during the night fifteen tons of supplies and concealed them in the bush. He spoke of the tremendous struggle he had had with himself on the beach. "Would he return with the boat or not?" He admitted that his nature shrank from the sacrifice, and with a sinking heart he stood on the beach and watched the boat that might have borne him to safety, sail out of the bay.

'After the departure of the boat, Fr Vivian had made his way quickly back to Sangara. He found the Japanese everywhere, and about to destroy the mission.

'When I arrived at the shelter there was quite a crowd of natives round about. Fr Vivian spoke to them thus: "I am your missionary. I have come back to you because I knew you would need your father. I am not going to run away from you. I am going to remain to help you as long as you will let me. To-morrow is Sunday. I shall say Mass, and any who wish may communicate." Shortly after dark he returned to the mission house to collect some church equipment. He returned about midnight and told me that as yet nothing had been touched in the mission, but the Japanese had told the people of their intention to destroy the place on the Sunday.

'Shortly after dawn he woke me up saying: "There is a big number of people here. I am going down to say Mass." He began to vest, and was nearly finished when a native boy rushed to us crying out: "Father! Doctor! Go; do not wait! During the night Embogi came and had a look at where you are, and has just gone to tell the Japanese, because he wants them to come and kill you."

'There was a dead silence. I looked at Fr Vivian. He bowed his head in prayer for a few moments, and then said to the people: "To-day is Sunday. It is God's day. I shall say Mass. We shall worship God. Why has Embogi done this? Does he hate us? Have we ever harmed him?" From here and there among the crowd came the reply: "Embogi is not a Christian".

'Turning to me, Fr Vivian said: "Will you remain for Mass?" "Yes" I said, and remained. I do not think I have ever witnessed a more devout congregation. The fervour expressed in those faces would have equalled that of the early Christians assisting at Mass in some hidden catacomb. Like those early Christians, these New Guinea Christians were assisting at Mass at the risk of their lives.

'The dense silence of the jungle was broken only by the sound of the priest's voice praying for his people. Then came the rustle of movement as those bare brown feet moved near the altar at the time of Communion. He who was about to go down to his own bitter Gethsemane and passion offered up for the last time before the throne of God for his people the saving Sacrifice of Christ. As the Sacrifice of Christ had its justification on Easter morning, so too in God's own time will the sacrifice of His loyal and devoted priest, Fr Redlich.

'After the Mass the people quietly dispersed. Fr Vivian and I moved on. The following day it became necessary for us to part. With sorrow not unmixed with a feeling of deep admiration for his courage, I bade him "Farewell and good luck!" He was going to remain with his people, moving about among them. My own duty bade me escape.'

Embogi came himself with his gang and captured Vivian along with the mission's nurse and teacher, Marjorie Brenchley and Lilla Lashmar, as they were trying to cross a river to a new hiding place. With them were Henry Holland, the priest, John Duffill the teacher and a Papuan Evangelist Lucian Tapiede from a neighbouring station of Isivita. Lucian tried to save his friends but Embogi had him killed there and then. The other five were handed over to the Japanese and beheaded on Buna Beach. Their bodies were thrown into the sea.

Vivian probably died on 6 August. Just over a week earlier he had written a letter to his father in England. He might almost have known it was to be his last.

'The war has busted up here', he wrote, 'I got back from Dogura and ran right into it, and am now somewhere in my parish trying to carry on, though my people are horribly scared. No news of May, I'm cut off from contacting her—my staff OK so far but at another spot.

'I am trying to stick whatever happens. If I don't come out of it, just rest content that I have tried to do my job faithfully.'

May that he speaks about was his fiancée, May Hayman; they had only been engaged a month. She was an Australian nurse who had trained at a hospital in Canberra. She joined the staff of the Church in New Guinea in 1936 and by 1941 was matron of the mission hospital at Gona. On Boxing Day of that year the Australian Government ordered all its nationals to leave New Guinea, but it allowed missionaries to remain if they wished. Along with Mavis Parkinson, also an Australian, a teacher who came from St Paul's parish, Ipswich in Queensland, May chose to remain at Gona.

On 21 July the Japanese bombarded Gona preparatory to a landing. The mission priest together with May and Mavis and a small group of Papuans, fled into the jungle. They eventually ran into a Japanese ambush at Popondetta. The priest became separated from the party, he wandering in one direction and they in another. Late in August the women were found by unfriendly Papuans and betrayed to the Japanese. One of the soldiers tried to assault Mavis and when she resisted he bayonetted her to death. May too was killed.

The Anglican Church in Australia commemorates eleven New Guinea martyrs together on 2 September and with them it also remembers in thanksgiving 15 Lutheran, 24 Methodist and 188 Roman Catholic Christians who died for their faith in New Guinea, New Britain and the Solomon Isles during World War Two.

Anglicans not so far mentioned are the Australian Henry Matthews who was the priest at Port Moresby and his Papuan Evangelist Leslie Gariadi. They died when a Japanese submarine attacked the boat in which they were taking a group of people to safety to Daru. John Barge, a priest from Queensland who was working on the neighbouring island of New Britain was killed at much the same time and a year later Bernard Moore from Leicestershire in England also stationed in New Britain, refused to leave his people and died of food poisoning in the jungle where he was in hiding.

Among the Roman Catholic Martyrs were fourteen brothers of the Society of the Divine Word, eighteen sisters from the Missionary Sisters, Servants of the

Holy Spirit, their Bishop, himself a member of the Society of the Divine Word, and six other priests. They were based at Wewak on the Northern coast of New Guinea over 400 miles from Buna. The Japanese military authorities were convinced that information about their troop and ship movements were being radioed to the Allies and accused the Missionaries of being responsible. As the majority of the brothers and sisters were Germans, they had imagined when war broke out they would be well treated by Japan, and were not a little surprised by the Japanese attitude. Bishop Joseph Loerks and the staff of the Wewak Mission were forced to board the Japanese ship Akikaze, under the impression that they were being deported. Later that day, 17 March 1943, the boat put in to Luga and took on more Catholic priests and missionary sisters, and some Protestant missionaries. The ship then sailed into open waters, a kind of gallows was set up and one by one the missionaries, blindfolded, their hands tied together, were hoisted up by their hands and shot. Their bodies were dropped straight into the sea.

PRAYER: *Lord keep me faithful, whatever happens.*

The names of all the Anglican martyrs mentioned appear in the Book of Modern Martyrs kept in St Paul's Cathedral, London.

Martyrs in Turkey 1909, 1913, 1922

(9 SEPTEMBER)

During his sermon on 9 September 1922, Metropolitan Chrysostom in Istanbul told his flock, 'The true Christian is revealed through tribulations'. He must have taken that deliberately as his theme for he knew that Turkish troops were on their way to the city to crush a riot that had broken out between the Greeks, mainly Orthodox Christians, and the Muslim Turks. Chrysostom had been given the chance to escape before the soldiers arrived, but he had refused to abandon his people. Later that evening he was arrested and handed over to the mob. After being beaten and trodden under foot he was dragged through the streets until he died. Doubtless his murderers saw him as a representative of the religious hierarchy of their age-long enemies, and an infidel; his fellow countrymen as another Greek victim of Turkish aggression; but to his fellow Christians he is yet another martyr.

Thirteen years earlier, this time in mainland Turkey, a young American, David Miner Rogers had been killed at Adana on 15 April 1909. David was born in New Britain, Connecticut, in 1882. Two years after he had left Hertford Seminary, he was sent to a Christian Mission at Hadjin, where his talents gave promise of very useful work, but he was killed during a wholesale massacre of Armenians, a group of Christians of very ancient origin in the Middle East, after only a few months of service.

Two years after David Rogers' death another young American arrived at Sivas. Charles Harding Holbrook came from Salem in Massachusetts and when he left the Union Seminary, New York in 1910 it was said of him that he was one of the most capable, best equipped and most promising missionaries ever to be trained there. He was well aware of the dangers he might have to face. In a letter to a friend just before he sailed he said 'I expect hardship, suffering and peril . . . I fear no evil and shall rejoice if I am accounted worthy to suffer for him'. He had only been at his post for about two years when he was murdered on 13 August 1913 in isolated hill country near to Sivas while he was touring with a native teacher.

PRAYER: *Holy Spirit make me glad to share in the sufferings of Christ.*

* * * * *

Winnie Letts   1907–1972

(20 SEPTEMBER)

William Sangster always used to say that every local congregation had its saint. In his biography of his father Paul Sangster mentions several of the saints in his father's congregations in various towns. Winnie Letts is not one of those but a saint nonetheless of a congregation that the author of this book used to serve. Every Sunday morning Winnie would be found in her wheel chair worshipping with the very small congregation on a modern housing estate in Northampton. She was badly crippled with arthritis and it used to take her three hours to get ready for a service which began at eleven. When the deacon was to be ordained priest in Peterborough Cathedral, she got up at five o'clock to be in time for the coach. Winnie was in constant pain, but she rarely complained and her serene trust in God shone in her face. Once at a Bible study her calm acceptance of suffering was a marvellous witness to the cross and a salutory shock to the rest of the group.

Winnie was born in Northampton. Her father died when she was very young and her mother remarried but this second husband died by the time Winnie was in her teens. Winnie's first job was in a box making factory but later she moved to Northampton's traditional trade of manufacturing boots and shoes. In 1947 she left home, went to London and got herself a job as linen-mistress at Great Ormond Street Hospital. At the same time she began to look after an ageing aunt and uncle. In 1950 she changed hospitals but five or so years later leg trouble developed and she had to give up hospital work. Soon it was necessary to give up going out to work altogether and she had to make boxes at home.

When she went on holiday to Weston-super-Mare in 1963 she met Monty Letts, an old friend of hers whose wife, also an old friend, had recently died. Winnie married Monty but within two years of her wedding, her husband had a stroke. Almost an invalid herself she looked after him pushing him around in a chair while she herself could hardly walk. She had to get him up in the morning and help him back to bed at night.

By 1968 she was becoming more and more incapable, and eventually Monty had to go into hospital. They spent a last Christmas Day together in December 1971, and died within seven months of each other the following year. Was there ever a more unpromising background for a joyful Christian? Winnie was always joyful and her memory is still fresh within her congregation. Perhaps one of the happiest memories will

be of Winnie being pushed in her wheel chair round
the estate for the Palm Sunday procession, her Palm
Cross and green branch on her lap, singing lustily for
the world to hear, 'All glory laud and honour', to her
Redeemer King. Winnie has her place in this book as
just one of the countless number of Saints, unknown
to the Church on earth at large, but beloved of God.
'Those here have been recorded in order that you may
hold the faith, that Jesus is the Christ, The Son of God,
and that through this faith you may possess eternal life
by His name' (John 20.31).

PRAYER: *Open my lips, O Lord, that my mouth may
proclaim your praise (Psalm 51.15).*

* * * * *

Alfred Lionel Sadd   1909–1942
and Companion Martyr

(15 OCTOBER)

The root meaning of the Hebrew word translated in
Greek by *'martyr'* was the verb 'to return' or 'to repeat'.
A Christian martyr repeated, either by his life or his
report, the life, death and resurrection of Jesus Christ.
In the New Testament all the apostles are called
martyrs, though the word is usually translated into
English as 'witnesses'. Over the years, martyr has
come to mean, not only a witness to the truth of the
gospel, but also one who dies for the sake of that truth,
and it is there that difficulties begin. It is clear in the

New Testament that Stephen died because of his faith in Jesus. So did James. Tradition has it that all of the Apostles apart from John, met unpleasant ends, and this has been the fate of many Christians through the centuries.

Some of these martyrs were given a simple choice like Polycarp's in the second century. Deny Christ and live; Confess Him and die. But many more had a different choice. Remain where I believe I am doing God's will or run away to safety. In colonial situations Christianity was or is often presented by Nationalists as the white man's religion. Persecution of native Christians can then be seen not in religious but political terms. Being a Christian is regarded as tantamount to being a traitor to the Nationalist cause. The Kikuyu martyrs in Kenya are very good examples.

Alfred Sadd is an example of those Christians who in times of war stay at their posts and take their chances under enemy occupation. He was attached to the London Missionary Society and had been sent by them first to Fiji and from there to the little island of Beru in the Kingsmill group of the Gilbert Islands. These islands though in part self-governing were still British colonies which made them obvious targets for the Japanese in World War Two.

Alfred arrived in Fiji in 1933. The Christians whom he served were scattered over hundreds of miles and the mission headquarters at Suva maintained contact through a succession of ships all named after John Williams. Williams was also a member of the London Missionary Society who was killed in November 1839, at Dillon's Bay, Erromanga in the New Hebrides group of islands. Alfred had been born and brought up among ships, and was never happier than when messing about in a boat. That alone made him an ideal member of the staff at Suva.

As soon as he had mastered the rudiments of their language, which he did in a remarkably short time, Alfred travelled in 'John Williams V' to Beru and began work. His letters home show him deeply involved in teaching, running a scout troop, home-building as well as repairing roofs, boats and radio equipment, in surgery, helping in the translating of parts of the Bible into a native dialect and of course his job as a Minister. For transport he often rode a bicycle which was tied together in places with bits of string and rattled and groaned in every joint. He had been ordained in his home church in Essex, Maldon Congregational Church. As a boy, Alfred had been sent from Maldon to The Leys School in Cambridge. One of his teachers still remembers him as a happy, friendly, good-natured boy, fond of fun, liked by everybody and up to various pranks, but the letters Alfred wrote as a young man reveal his difficulties with English spelling. Phenomena he spelt *phenomina*; he was unable to distinguish between *berth* and *birth* and once wrote about a *new commer's* impression of his work in Beru.

One of his friends said of him, 'his writing is illegible, his spelling original and his punctuation erratic, but he is of the salt of the earth'. His headmaster had once written much the same for although he regretted his lack of academic success he considered Alfred to be 'one of the greatest influences for good' in the school.

In 1942 the Japanese began to occupy the Gilbert Islands. Alfred, along with other British subjects, was given the opportunity of leaving, but he decided to stay. In a letter soon after February of that year he said 'I have a feeling that God has something bigger than this he intends me to do. I hope and pray I shall be found faithful.' He was. In August 1942 the Japanese came to Rongorrongo in Beru. The natives were gathered at bayonet point into Alfred's Church. Alfred himself was arrested, his captors having tried to make him walk on the Union Jack, his own national flag. He and five other Europeans were taken to another island in the group, Tarawa, and there beheaded.

The Japanese killed him because he was a patriotic Englishman. He and the Roman Catholic priest who died with him were in the Gilbert Islands because they were Christians, witnesses to the Gospel of Christ.

PRAYER: *In you Lord I trust and shall not be afraid what man can do to me (Psalm 56.11).*

* * * * *

Orthodox Confessors and Martyrs in Russia   1931, 1941, 1962

(28 OCTOBER)

The separation of Church from State is not as simple as it might appear. In the early days of the Church it was comparatively easy for the State to ignore the Church, but as soon as it looked as though Christ's claims on men were going to conflict with the claims of Caesar, Caesar had to take notice. Persecution is invariably tried first. If attack doesn't work, and we have our Lord's promise that it never will work, State and Church have to learn to live together in what can sometimes be a very uneasy tension.

Church/State relations in Russia after the Revolution followed the general pattern. The Tsarist government had always kept a tight control over the Orthodox Church and as a result the Church was seen by the Revolutionaries as a conservative influence, dedicated to the Imperial Government, and opposed to all that Communists stood for. The majority of the Communist party were in fact atheists who believed that the Church was one of the last bastions of feudal privilege, helping to keep the proletariat contented in their poverty by promise of felicity in the world to come.

In the 1920s the revolutionary Government was still convinced that the abolition of religion would be a simple matter. In 1987 they know too well that despite frequent persecutions the Orthodox Church and other Christian groups in Russia are still very strong—and not simply amongst the old folk.

Not many years after the overthrow of the Tsar the Soviet Government managed to engineer a schism within the Russian Church, between those who were prepared to compromise and therefore become totally subservient to the secular authorities and those who weren't. Large numbers of bishops and priests supported the schismatics under the impression that only in that way the Church could be preserved from complete extinction. Among those not prepared to compromise were Michael Alexandrovich Zhizhilenko, Sophia Grineva, and Bishop Afansay Sakharov.

Michael Zhizhilenko was a physician and psychiatrist, and became Medical Superintendent of the Tanganka prison in Moscow. He was a great friend of Patriarch Tikhon who wore himself out, undergoing much suffering and imprisonment, in trying to defend the Church against the government. The Patriarch persuaded Michael to become a priest and to take the vows of a monk secretly so that the Church's ministry should survive in the event of an all out persecution, and two years after the Patriarch's death, Michael was secretly consecrated Bishop of Serpukhov. He was first arrested in 1929 and sent to the Solovki Labour Camp. Here with other Orthodox Christians the Liturgy was secretly celebrated, sometimes in the nearby forests and sometimes in one of the cells. Michael was eventually shot on 6 July 1931.

Sophia Grineva was Abbess of a small community of nuns. She was imprisoned several times between the Revolution and 1927. With about twenty of her sisters she refused to acknowledge the authority of the state supported Bishops, and left the convent in Kiev to live the Religious life in secret. During her last imprisonment her health suffered greatly but she died surrounded by her sisters on 4 April 1941.

Bishop Afanasy also withstood the state recognized ecclesiastical authorities. For this he was arrested for the first time on 15 June 1922. In 1954 when he was celebrating the thirty-third anniversary of his consecration as Bishop he recalled that during those years he had spent thirty-three months in his diocese carrying out his duties, and a further thirty-two in the diocese forbidden to do his work. Just over six years was spent in exile and a little over twenty-one years either in prison or hard labour camps.

In a letter before his final release in 1955 from the Temnikov concentration camp he wrote,

'There is no change in my circumstances I sit near the sea and wait on the weather. I look at this calmly in the firm knowledge that our fate depends not on earthly rulers but on him who holds in his hands the fate of rulers . . . Let the Lord's will be done. Glory to God for everything.' He was eventually freed from all penal restraint in 1955 and returned to live in semi-retirement near his old diocese, working on liturgical texts for the then Patriarch of Moscow. The schism within the Orthodox Church in Russia came to an end soon after the German invasion of Russia in World War Two thus enabling Afanasy to be reconciled with The Patriarchate.

In 1973 a short biography of the Bishop in Russian, written by someone living in the Soviet Union, was published in Paris. The unknown author describes Afanasy's last days on earth, in 1962 after an illness of some months.

'The next day, Friday evening, he was able to say clearly "Prayer will save us all". Then he wrote with his fingers on the blanket, "Save, O Lord". When he was asked to write something else, he drew in large letters "FINISHED" and added a full stop.' He spoke no more and died on the Sunday, 28 October.

PRAYER: *Glory to God for everything.*

Michael Alexandrovich Zhizhilenko, Sophia Grineva together with Patriarch Tikhon and many others are revered by the Synodical Russian Orthodox Church outside Russia as Martyrs.

* * * * *

Anastassios Kephalas   1846–1920
(Nectarios of Pentapolis)
(21 NOVEMBER)

Anastassios Kephalas was born in Selyvria in Eastern Thrace in 1846. Because of the poverty of his family he went to Istanbul at 14 to work as a clerk in a tobacco merchant's store. In that city he was able to read books on the Christian Faith and the spiritual life, to attend church regularly, and to pray. With his earnings he tried to help support his parents.

His employer under-paid him and so the young lad went about poorly dressed and bare-foot. Anastassios noticed that his employer wrote and received many letters, and he too wanted to write a letter. But to whom could he write? He had no friends in Istanbul and it was useless to write to his mother because she couldn't read. In all he was thoroughly miserable. Throughout this period he never lost faith in God, and one day he thought of writing a letter to his Saviour and telling Him about his troubles. He found a pencil and wrote:

My little Christ—I do not have an apron or shoes. You send them to me. You know how much I love you. Anastassios.

He put it in an envelope and addressed it to 'The Lord Jesus Christ in Heaven'. On his way to post the letter he met a neighbouring merchant who also had some letters. He offered to post the one Anastassios was holding and at the Post Office the merchant happened to notice the address on Anastassios' letter. He was thunderstruck, and opened and read it. The letter surprised him more than the address. His heart was touched and he sent the boy some money at once.

Although he had not had much by way of formal education Anastassios was a voracious reader and in his late teens he was able to leave his master and become an overseer of children in an Orthodox Church School in Istanbul. When he was twenty he left that city and was appointed a school teacher on the island of Chios. He taught in that school for seven years but all the time was becoming increasingly attracted to the life of a monk and on 7 November 1875 he took his vows at the monastery of Nea Moni on Chios.

Two years later the Bishop made him a deacon and named him Nectarios. With the support of Patriarch Sophroni of Alexandria, Nectarios was able to enter Athens University. In 1885 he went to Egypt and was ordained priest and in 1889 he was consecrated Bishop becoming Metroplitan of Pentapolis. He was much loved for his obvious sanctity and sad though it is to have to admit it, his fellow bishops became very jealous of him. In their spite they persuaded the Patriarch that Nectarios was a hypocrite and had designs on the Patriarch's job. He was convinced by their lies, and suspended Nectarios from his diocese though he did allow him to officiate at services provided he always had the permission of the local bishop.

Nectarios submitted to the disgrace humbly, but his flock were not so pleased about it and began to demand to know the reason for the Patriarch's action. To prevent further squabbles Nectarios exiled himself to Greece.

He arrived in Athens penniless and with a letter which gave as an explanation of his suspension 'reasons known to the Patriarch.' He was, not surprisingly, greeted by both Church and State officials with distrust and downright hostility. It is well to remember that in Greece in those days while the State always tried to keep tight control of the Church, the Church authorities were not above political manoeuvring themselves. Nobody would help Nectarios or give him work. He was destitute, without food or money and was forced to beg outside the office of the Minister of Religion. One day he met an acquaintance from his days in Egypt. The friend was surprised to see

Nectarios in such a state and helped him to an appointment as a preacher in the diocese of Vitineia and Eubioea. Nectarios, grateful to be allowed to preach the Word of God again, set sail at once for the Island of Euboiea and joyfully began his work but rumours followed him there and he was forced to return to Athens.

By now his true worth was beginning to be recognized and Nectarios was appointed Dean of the Rizarium Seminary in Athens in 1894. There he was able to teach the students, and officiate at Divine worship. The seminary had previously been in a state of turmoil and anarchy but Nectarios by his very presence restored peace and order.

In 1908 he resigned from the seminary and went to the island of Aegina, where, in a ruined church dedicated to the Most Holy Trinity, he founded a convent. The church was rebuilt by Nectarios and his faithful companion Xenia, a blind nun who later became Superior of the Community.

Gifts were so abundant that soon the community was able to build more cells and increase its numbers to 30. Once, while the building was in progress, a very rich woman from Athens arrived with a donation of 3,000 drachmas! 'I am grateful to you for your effort but I cannot receive the money', said Nectarios. He went on, 'The reason is that you have quarrelled with many people and it's your fault. Stay here and rest yourself; afterwards go and be reconciled with your friends and relatives; then return with your gift'. The woman was speechless but she did as she was told and within three months she was back. Nectarios accepted her gift.

In September 1920 Nectarios became very ill. Despite his protests he was taken to a hospital in Athens and admitted to the pauper's ward. The hospital authorities refused at first to believe that this little, penniless old monk was a bishop though round his neck they found a small ikon of Mary, Mother of God, traditionally worn by Orthodox bishops. For two months he suffered terrible pains and died on 21 November.

PRAYER: *To love you Lord I must love my fellows. Forgive me when I fail.*

Nectarios has been canonised by the Orthodox Church in Greece.

*   *   *   *   *

Chundra Lela   c 1840–1907

(26 NOVEMBER)

To have an unmarried daughter was for Hindu parents a great disgrace, so it is perhaps not surprising that Chundra Lela was married at seven years old. The marriage was arranged by her parents, and because her father was a Brahmin attached to the court of the King of Nepal she had to marry a priest. In all probability she lived in the capital Kathmandu which lies 60 miles south west of the most famous mountain in Nepal, Everest.

If marriage at seven seems unpleasant (of course she was not expected to live with her husband until both were considered adult), widowhood at nine when her boy husband died, was an absolute disaster, for although the Hindu scriptures do not actually forbid remarriage, it had nevertheless become expected of a widow in Chundra Lela's day that she should spend her remaining years in seclusion, mourning the death of her husband.

Although Chundra's father had followed the custom of finding an early husband for his child, in another respect he was very unconventional, especially when he began to educate his young daughter as a Brahmin by teaching her to read, not only her own language, but also Sanskrit, the ancient language of India in which the Hindu scriptures are largely written.

When she was thirteen her father decided to go on pilgrimage to the shrine of the God Jagannatha at Puri on the East Coast of India. Jagannatha, also known as Juggernaut, is one of the several forms under which the God Krishna is worshipped. His shrine in Puri is particularly famous for the annual 'car festival' in the summer when his image is placed on a chariot or car so heavy that hundreds of men and women are needed to pull it.

He is taken to his 'country house' accompanied by vast crowds of worshippers and it was even known for some of them in their fervour to throw themselves under the chariot and so be crushed to death. The effect of all this on a girl of thirteen must be left to the imagination.

Chundra's mother was dead but another tragedy was to follow, for her father died while they were in Puri, leaving her an orphan.

As in many religions, Hinduism teaches that personal catastrophes including widowhood are the result of sin and when she returned to Nepal, Chundra read in her sacred books that the sin which had caused her to lose her husband could be forgiven if she carried out certain religious obligations, which included worshipping at the four great shrines of

India. One of these was the very temple at Puri where her father died. With two servants and the gold she had received as a legacy from her husband, she slipped out of the town at night to begin the 550 mile journey to Puri. She stayed at the temple a fortnight, praying, laying on feasts for the Brahmins who served at the shrine, buying a cow to provide them with milk and making expensive offerings to the god.

From Puri she went further south to Pamban Island, about twenty miles from Ceylon, to the temple built on the spot where Ram, with the help of the Monkey God Hanuman, was said to have been reunited with his beautiful wife Sita. Chundra worshipped here for ten days, feeding the priests as at Puri. It was here that she took Ram as her patron, always carrying with her an image of him which she had bought at his temple.

For the third shrine she had to travel over 1,000 miles to the North West. It must have taken several years for her to arrive at the temple of Krishna at Dwarka, The City of Many Gates. Here Krishna died and Hindus believed that a visit to Dwarka released the pilgrim from sin. Chundra stayed for another fortnight and then wearily set her face to go still farther North, nearly another 1,000 miles to the last of the four shrines, that of the god Vishnu at Badrinath, 14,000 feet up in the Himalayas. In indescribable suffering she and her two faithful servants climbed the snow covered mountain in their bare feet, and remained in the temple for five days, their raw feet wrapped in old clothes. The whole pilgrimage had taken seven years, but still Chundra remained dissatisfied. She had not yet found the peace of God.

She visited yet more holy places including Benares where every day thousands of pilgrims struggle to bathe in the sacred river, the Ganges. Here her two servants died of the ever prevalent cholera and Chundra was alone, unsure of where she should go

next until she met a band of pilgrims on their way to
Puri who allowed her to join them. At Puri she lived
with her new companions in a place which had been
built for pilgrims by the ruler of the area. Each day the
King sent servants with food for them, but he was
astonished when his servant told him about a woman
who had proudly refused his food while she sat
reading her sacred books. He could hardly believe his
ears. A woman being able to read or a pilgrim refusing
gifts of food was almost unheard of. Chundra was
summoned to the Royal presence. She told the King
and Queen of her search for God and when she
revealed that she was a Brahmin's daughter she was
promptly invited to become priestess to the court.

Chundra remained with that family for seven years,
acting as priest for their worship, teaching the women
Sanskrit and learning two more languages herself.
Such is the respect that Hindus have for their holy
men and women, she herself was treated almost as if
she were divine, but she remained restless, her thirst
for God unquenched.

Her religion held out one last hope, albeit a terrify-
ing one. Once again she set out on her pilgrimage from
shrine to shrine only this time she intended to subject
her body to the most incredible torments. This she
imagined would please the gods. She became a fakir,
disfiguring her face with ashes and paint and matting
her hair with cowdung. During the six hot months of
the year she sat in the burning sun with five fires
surrounding her, imploring her god to reveal himself.
In winter months she changed the penance, sitting
through the night in a pond with the water up to her
neck, telling her rosary of 108 beads.

For three years she persecuted her body. Wearily at
the end of her trials she went to Calcutta, to cut off her
long matted hair and throw it as an offering into the
Ganges. Surely she had suffered all that could be

required of any human being? Would she not now see God?

In every religion some unscrupulous priests have fooled devotees with weeping statues, liquefying blood, and similar 'miracles'. The discovery of such frauds can shatter the faith of believers, and when Chundra Lela found a priest dipping cloth in blood, not from the statue of a god from which it was supposed to have flowed, but from the carcass of a pig the priest had killed, her doubts began. Soon she had accumulated plenty of evidence that many Brahmins were using the simplicity of the faithful to feather their own nests.

At Midnapur, 50 miles to the west of Calcutta, she settled down as a guru, surrounded by a number of disciples whom, sitting by the roadside, she taught to read their scriptures and say their prayers. It was customary for the more well to do women to ask a holy woman to come to their homes to read to them, and Chundra pleased one family so much that they built a room for her on to their own house. All the time Chundra was becoming more and more disillusioned with her religion to the point of giving away her collection of images of the gods. She spent more time with the family and one day found one of them reading some Christian literature. Chundra was only too ready for new books and new ideas. She bought a bible and it was not long before she was yet again surrounded by eager disciples only this time she was using the Christian Scriptures as her text book. She had come to the end of her search. Soon she was asking for Baptism.

In her search for God, Chundra had spent nearly twenty years wandering throughout India, journeying from shrine to shrine, convinced that only through her own exertions, bodily and spiritual, could she discover God and receive forgiveness. As a Christian she spent the rest of her life, over thirty five years, still wandering, often from shrine to shrine, preaching that God was in Jesus Christ reconciling the world to himself. Forgiveness is for free.

She was much like Francis of Assisi. She would rely for food on the compassion of those she met. She travelled light and once in wintertime when she had been given a blanket by a fellow Christian she said 'Just see how my friends trouble me. How can a travelling fakir be burdened with such a bundle?'

Her friends were to trouble her further. As she got older they wanted to build her a house for her to die in. She didn't like the idea much. 'Do you know where I am to die? It might be in the distant jungle or perhaps while preaching in the street.' Undeterred they chose the site, a peaceful spot under the mango trees, but when she saw it she wouldn't have it. If they must build her a house then she wanted it on the roadside, 'so that when I am too old and weak I may crawl up to the door and preach to the people as they pass by'. She had her way. The woman who had once spent days in front of scorching fires or nights up to her neck in cold water, was not to be prevented even in old age from proclaiming the One she had found.

As for her new home, she was soon sharing it with a poor disgraced Hindu woman and her child, and it was this woman who cared for Chundra in her last severe illness. She died there on 26 November 1907 whispering to her new friend, 'All is bright. I have no fear. Look at the messengers who have come to carry me up to God.' As an old Mohammedan said at her funeral, 'A holy life, a holy life'.

PRAYER: *Bless the Lord, my soul, forget none of his benefits (Psalm 103.2).*

Charles de Foucauld   1858–1916

(1 DECEMBER)

It is hard to believe that a man who lived in a gardener's hut in the grounds of a convent in Nazareth, ate a small meal at midday of milk, soup, figs and honey and an evening meal of only a small piece of bread could possibly have been the same man who at eighteen just avoided being rejected for the élite Military Academy of St Cyr in France, because he was too fat. As a young aristocrat Charles had a reputation for enjoying good food and of being a bit of a rake. He was so used to high living and having his own way that he even resigned his commission in 1881 because his superior officers insisted that he should send Mimi, his mistress, back to France. He refused, left the army and set up house with Mimi at Evian on the shores of Lake Geneva. It lasted no more than three months. Charles' regiment was in action in Algeria and he hurried back to Paris. Nothing more is heard of Mimi. He remained a soldier at heart all his life; he merely changed his Commander-in-chief.

Charles claimed to have given up belief in God and the practice of his religion at a fairly early age, yet later when he wrote about his wild oats he said, 'I committed evil, but I neither liked it nor approved what I was doing. And you, Lord, would make me feel an emptiness, a despondency such as I have experienced at no other time but then . . . It would come back every night when I found myself alone again in my flat. I continued to arrange my parties, but once they started, I would go through them with infinite boredom and sickening disgust'.

At the age of twenty-five he undertook to explore Morocco, at that time a country of great mystery into which Europeans were never admitted. Dressed as a Moroccan Jew and claiming to be a rabbi from Central Europe, he travelled through the greater part of the land for about eighteen months with a genuine rabbi as his guide. The expedition was rife with adventure, and more than once Charles risked his life, displaying great courage and endurance. On his return to France he published a description of his journeys, including his scientific observations. The book was an immediate success, but by then he had lost interest in it. In the desert and through his contacts with the Muslim Arabs he had glimpsed something of the greatness of God.

He was trying to pray again, and found himself going on his knees in various churches. His prayer was quite simple, 'O God, if you exist, let me know of your existence'. Did he not know the words of a famous fellow-countryman Blaise Pascal? He pictures God as saying to one who is searching for Him, 'Comfort yourself, you would not seek me if you had not found me' (*Pensées Sect. vii 533*).

Charles later wrote of four blessings our Lord had given him. These included the example of a Christian friend, a desire to discover the truth in Christianity and the actual study of the faith. The fourth was being sent for instruction in religion to Father Huvelin, the priest of St Augustine's Church in Paris. 'I believe, O God, that by teaching me to go into his confessional on one of the last days of that October . . . you were giving me the best of all good things. If there is joy in heaven over the repentence of a sinner, then how great joy there must have been when I entered the confessional.'

Charles was incapable of half-measures. 'The moment I realised that God existed,' he wrote some time later to another soldier, 'I knew I could not do otherwise than to live for him alone.' He wanted desperately to live like Jesus, and for seven years he lived as a Trappist Monk, the severest and most austere Religious Order in the Catholic Church, but for Charles even they were too comfortable. He yearned for what he thought of as the insecure years that Jesus lived in a poor home in Nazareth. It is open to question whether our Lord actually was so poor at home, but he certainly said during his ministry that he hadn't anywhere then to lay his head. Charles was allowed to leave the Trappists and he went to the Holy Land and settled in that garden hut belonging to some nuns called Poor Clares at Nazareth. His clothes were rather peculiar and he was mocked and sometimes even stoned by the local children but he was happy, for he was literally sharing the lot of Jesus Christ, whom he loved so dearly.

Charles spent two years of silence and prayer in the Holy Land. For hours at a time he would remain on his knees motionless in the sisters' chapel, and whatever free time he had from the work the sisters gave him, he would devote to thinking about God as he reveals himself in the Bible. Charles was convinced that one day he would have brothers to share this life with him, and an immense desire grew in him to bring the Gospel to the poorest and most forsaken people. He wanted his 'Little Brothers' as in his imagination he called them, to be apostles not so much by their preaching as by their entire lives. He wanted them to observe literally the command of Jesus to 'take the lowest place' and it was this that made him refuse ordination as a priest for a long time.

He was eventually ordained, and was anxious to go to Morocco, where he had not found a single priest during his earlier expeditions. This time of course he wanted to go quite openly, but permission was refused and he finally settled down at Tamanrasset, in the very heart of the Sahara. The village is the centre for a tribe of people called Touareg. Charles had a hut built for himself, similar to those in which the tribesmen lived. He began to visit them and asked them to his home, especially when they were sick. Their language had never been written down so he wrote a grammar and a dictionary, and made a collection of their traditional poems and proverbs. He also translated the Gospels for them. He worked extremely hard but would cheerfully allow himself to be interrupted at any time. The tiniest details of their lives concerned him and he once wrote to his cousin Marie in France to ask for some black dye for the women who were going grey. But he never quite forsook his military upbringing and frequently gave the French Colonial Army information that he picked up in the desert. This must have come to the notice of the guerillas who kept up a war of attrition with the French.

During the First World War little happened in the Sahara for two years but in 1916 trouble broke out. One day someone called out to Charles that the post had arrived. As he put out a hand for his letters, two Senouissis tribesmen, hostile to the French, dragged him out and bound him while a third shot him in the head.

He seems a failure. No brother had come to share his life, all his schemes had come to nothing. It was not until 1933 that the Little Brothers came into being, seventeen years after Charles' death. 'In truth, in very truth I tell you' says Jesus, 'A grain of wheat remains a solitary grain unless it falls into the ground and dies; but if it dies, it bears a rich harvest' (John 12.24). The Little Brothers now number over 200 from about 20 different nationalities, living in thirty different countries.

PRAYER: *My God I love you: My God I love you above all things.*

The cause for the canonisation of Charles de Foucauld was introduced at Rome in 1927. His Church has as yet made no further moves. Australian Anglicans, however, have added his name to their new calendar.

* * * * *

John and Betty Stam
1907/1906–1934
Margaret Morgan and Minka Hanskamp
1974
(9 DECEMBER)

'All Jesus' followers have to do, all they can do, is to lift up Christ before the world, bring him into dingy corners and dark places of the earth where he is unknown, introduce him to strangers, talk about him to everybody, and live so closely with and in him that others may see that there really is such a person as Jesus, because some being proves it by being like him.'

Betty Stam wrote that in a letter to her young brother when she was studying at the Moody Bible Institute in Chicago, USA. She not only wrote those words, she lived them. Betty had been born to American parents but brought up in China where her parents were missionaries, so it seemed quite natural that when she decided to offer herself as a missionary it was to China she wanted to go. She had met her husband John at the Bible Institute, but they had not

married until both were in China under the auspices of
the China Inland Mission.

A year after their marriage at Tsinan on the Yellow
River on 25 October 1933, they made their way south
to their future home and mission station at Tsingteh
about a hundred miles east of Anking on the Yangtze
River. China at that time was in the throes of what
amounted to a Civil War between Communists and
supporters of the republican regime known as
Nationalists who had achieved power after the overthrow of the Imperial Government. John knew that
there were Communist guerilla forces in the Tsingteh
area and since he now had a wife and baby daughter,
he made some enquiries of the civilian authorities, but
was assured by them that it was quite safe and that his
family would be protected.

They arrived at Tsingteh in November 1934 but
since they had few possessions they quickly settled in
their new home. As the Communist army foraged for
supplies, it was not long before rumours of rice-
stealing reaching their ears. They were not too surprised. John and Betty had both faced the possibility
that they would be killed in such unsettled times. Not
long before their arrival at Tsingteh John had written,

'In our lives it is well to remember that God's
supervision is so blessedly true that at any given
moment we may stop, and whether we face suffering or joy, times of intense activity and responsibility or times of rest and leisure, whatever we face we
may say, "For this cause came I unto this hour". All
of our social, church and family background, all of
our training, conscious and unconscious, has been
to prepare us to meet the present circumstances,
and to meet them to the glory of his name. This will
bring us to our tasks relieved of a shrinking that

would unnerve us, conscious of the fact that he who uses "a worm to thresh mountains" can use us too. "For this cause came I unto this hour. Father glorify thy name".'

Was it entirely coincidental that John had quoted the words of our Lord before His Passion? On the 6 December 1934 the Communist forces captured Tsing-teh. Crossing the mountains by unfrequented paths, they came in behind the government army, sixty miles to the south. With scarcely any warning, their advance guard scaled the city wall and threw open the gates. It was early morning. Betty was bathing their little daughter Helen when the first messenger came. Others followed quickly. The District Magistrate, after a short, ineffectual resistance, had fled, and before the Stams could escape, firing was heard on the streets—the looting of the city had begun.

John and Betty with their faithful servants knelt in prayer. They were perfectly composed, and even when the soldiers thundered at the door they opened to them with quiet courtesy. While John was talking with the leaders trying to satisfy their demands for goods and money, Betty actually served them with tea and cakes. But courtesy was as useless as resistance would have been. John was bound and carried off to the Communist headquarters, and before long they returned for Betty.

Their captors intended to use John and Betty as hostages. Their lives would be spared on payment of a vast sum of money. John was compelled to write to the Mission Headquarters. 'They want $20,000 before they will free us, which we have told them we are sure will not be paid. Famine relief money and our personal money and effects are all in their hands. God give you wisdom in all you do and give us grace and fortitude.

He is able.'

He was right, no money was sent. Next day, bound with ropes, their hands behind them, John and Betty were forced out into the streets. The guards called the townsfolk to come to see them die at the top of a hill outside the town. Before the execution the Communists harangued the unwilling spectators. Suddenly a native Christian doctor burst through the crowd and begged for their lives. He too was arrested and suffered death later when his Christian faith was discovered. John was beheaded first, followed by Betty. Their baby had inexplicably been left behind and was found in the empty house. Christian friends fled with her into the hills, and she was eventually handed over to the loving care of her mother's parents.

In March 1975 the police in Bankok found the bodies of Margaret Morgan and Minka Hamskamp in the mountains of South Thailand. Eleven months earlier on 23 April 1974 they too had been kidnapped, taken at gunpoint from their leprosy clinic in a village between the provincial capitals of Pattani and Yala in the largely Malay populated area of South Thailand. Their captors were bandits who for some time had been operating in that part of the country. A week later the Overseas Missionary Fellowship, formerly the China Inland Mission received a demand for a ransom of $500,000. As for John and Betty Stam, it was refused. Both of the nurses had known it would be.

Margaret was born at Porth, Rhondda in Wales in 1934. She trained as a nurse at Bristol and in 1964 joined the Fellowship and their work in South Thailand. It was not long after her arrival that the Mission began its village leprosy clinics in Thailand, operated from a base at Saiburi hospital on the coast.

Minka was living in the Dutch East Indies when World War II broke out and was interned by the

Japanese. After the war she emigrated to New Zealand but was back in Thailand, working in the Fellowship in 1958.

The Missionary Fellowship had some kind of contact with the two women four months after their capture, but thereafter heard nothing more. It can only be assumed that Margaret and Minka died in the service of our Lord sometime in September 1974.

PRAYER: *Father, glorify your Name in me.*

* * * * *

Ethel Tomkinson   1887–1967
(11 DECEMBER)

Ethel Tomkinson was as fond of spinach as Popeye. That and dry toast seem to have made up her staple diet during much of her fifty years of service to our Lord in the Church of India. Her simple diet was no fad but an attempt to live at a subsistence level similar to the poor whom she served at Mysore, Kastur and Mandagadde in South India.

Ethel was born and brought up in Colwyn Bay, a seaside town on the coast of North Wales. Even as a child she was concerned for missionaries so it can have come as no surprise to the family when in 1909 she began her training for the Deaconess Order in the Methodist Church at their College at Ilkley in Yorkshire. It was not enough. She wanted to be as fully qualified as was possible and so when she finished at Ilkley she began training as a nurse in Liverpool, and won a medal as one of the best students in her year. Just before the outbreak of World War I she sailed for

India, having been appointed nursing sister of the Mary Holdsworth Memorial Hospital of the Methodist Missionary Society at Mysore, where she remained for eighteen years.

Poverty exacerbates the danger of promiscuity. One way a girl can always earn a living is by selling her body, and that too often leads to venereal diseases which kill. Before she came to India Ethel had led a reasonably sheltered life, but in Mysore she was to see at close quarters the degradation to which, in appalling social circumstances, human kind so frequently sinks.

She had a particular gift for work among women and girls and so she was asked to leave the hospital and take charge of evangelistic work over an area of four hundred miles. She used as she said, 'to go and sit where the women sit, in their hovels; or it sometimes happens that they consider their dwellings too dirty . . . so a very grimy mat is spread in the street and we sit there and I tell them of the absolutely pure One who still comes to seek and save the lost'. Ether always tried to share the lives of those to whom she had come, hence that spinach. At seventy she looked a frail old lady, almost as thin as the undernourished villagers with whom she had completely identified herself.

It was while she was touring the villages in her circuit that she realised the need for a headquarters, not in a big town, but near where her people lived. India has for centuries been a very religious country and holy men of the Hindu faith have set up settlements on the edge of the jungle, away from the towns, where they and their disciples, living very simply, could mediate and serve all who came to them for help. Such a settlement is called an Ashram, and not surprisingly Christians have frequently begun Ashrams. Ethel did so first at Kastur and later at

Mandagadde. This latter site had been the place where twelve hundred years previously a Hindu Mystic had lived and prayed. The area was riddled with malaria and in our own era a hospital had been started, which lasted, but only just, for twenty years. During World War Two the army requisitioned the buildings as a training camp for jungle warfare and then a gaol. In 1949 when the buildings were returned to the church, Ethel offered to leave her Ashram at Kastur and set up a second at Mandagadde.

Not long after her arrival in Southern India, Christians, from various churches there had began to discuss the possibility of uniting into a single body. It took a long time but on 27 September 1947 the Church of South India was inaugurated and three churches, Anglican, Methodist and The United Church merged into one. Five years later in 1952 Ethel became one of the first sisters in the Order for Women in the Church of South India. It added a further dimension to her life, leading her to a deep longing for the total re-union of Christendom.

When she eventually retired from her work in India she returned to England and became one of the founder members of the Farncombe Community, who dedicated themselves to a life of prayer for the unity of the Church. Increasing frailty compelled her departure from the Community's house, but after a few months at the home for retired deaconesses at Grimsby she accepted gratefully an invitation to join Dr Cicely Saunders in London in the then newly founded St Christopher's Hospice for the care of the dying where her prayers, her radiant presence and her steadfast faith helped many to overcome the terrors of death. She herself died there on 11 December 1967.

PRAYER: *Jesus I am yours: you will not lose me.*

Frances Xavier Cabrini 1850–1917

(22 DECEMBER)

The Chicago train from Seattle had been attacked by train wreckers. A violent explosion shattered the windows of the carriage in which Maria Francesca Cabrini was sitting, and a huge iron bolt skimmed over the top of her head. The Railway officials scrambled into the carriage to find Maria unscathed. The guard whistled in surprise as he looked at her Nun's habit and exclaimed, 'Sure, someone was looking after you sister'. It had been like that throughout her life. As a girl she had fallen into a river and nobody, not even Maria herself, could say how she had got to the bank in safety.

The year was 1906, and Maria, or rather Mother Frances Xavier Cabrini as she was then called, had eleven more years in front of her. She was 56, but the really important part of her life's work had been completed. It is true that in 1910 at a time when she was trying to resign as superior of the congregation of Sisters she had founded she was in fact installed in that office for life, and this sign of the love and affection in which she was held by her community touched her deeply, but by then her congregation had kept its silver jubilee, and was firmly established in schools, orphanages, students' hostels and hospitals in eight different countries. Despite this diversity it is in America she is best remembered and when she was declared a Saint by Pope Pius XII she became the first citizen of the United States (she was naturalised in 1909) to be canonised by the Roman Catholic Church.

She had been born an Italian. Her parents were quite well off, but from her earliest years Maria had developed a passion for missionaries. She was quite convinced that she would be a missionary sister herself and wanted to go to China.

Like her elder sister, Rosa, who had been responsible for Maria Francesca's earlier education, she trained as a teacher, but when she applied to enter a community of Missionary Nuns she was turned down on the grounds of poor health. The real reason seems to have been her skill as a teacher; the priests in whose parishes she worked did not want to lose her. One of them however was promoted to an important post in Codogno and at his suggestion, the Bishop of that area asked her to sort out a rather peculiar orphanage in the town. At first she refused, but eventually was persuaded to take it on. For six years she tried to bring order to the orphanage and the lives of those who were responsible for it, but in the end she had to leave and with her went seven novices who although finding the orphanage impossible had been drawn to follow Maria Francesca. They shared her desire to become Missionaries and together in a disused Friary in Codogno they founded the Missionary Sisters of the Sacred Heart.

Mother Francesca had a hard time in persuading the Church authorities to recognise them. She still wanted to go to China but several of her friends suggested that the people who needed her and her sisters most were the Italian Immigrants in the United States. The Archbishop of New York invited her to work in his diocese. She decided to ask the Pope for his orders. Leo XIII, who was to be her friend for the rest of her life, well aware of the awful conditions in which many of the immigrants lived, said to her, 'Not East, but to the West. Go to the United States.'

She lost no time and with seven sisters set sail from Le Havre on 23 March 1889. She had received a promise of a house in New York so that the sisters could begin an orphanage and school immediately. When they arrived after a journey that they had not enjoyed, they discovered that the house was not available after all. The next morning they could hardly believe their ears when they heard the Archbishop suggesting that they should return to Italy by the next boat. He seems to have been a somewhat vacillating character but in Mother Cabrini he had met his match. She insisted that they had been sent to America by the Pope to do a job and she intended to do it. Reluctantly the Archbishop agreed. He could offer little help, but on 8 May she and her sisters took into their care their first children from the Italian community in New York where the sisters quickly discovered that many families who, in the land of their birth would have been devout Christians, had long ceased going to church.

Francesca also opened a day-school in the Italian Church, but it was a far from satisfactory arrangement and periodically everyone had to be turned out for a funeral or a wedding. The sisters began systematic visiting of the whole area and saw for themselves the horrifying conditions in which the immigrants lived. Francesca was anxious that they should live among the people they were wanting to serve, and eventually a dilapidated house which could serve as both a convent and school was found. To begin with the sisters had a few beds but no bed clothes, and no means of earning their living, but the people were overjoyed that some Italian sisters had at last come to live among them, and treated them with that generosity which is always to be found among the poor.

In July Mother Cabrini returned to Italy to report the progress of their work in America and to visit her congregation's houses in Europe. It was to be the first of many round trips she was to make. She was constantly on the move, investigating the possibilities of new work throughout the United States and various South American republics. To begin with the work had been amongst Italian immigrants, and had taken the forms of orphanages, schools for the poor, and fee-paying schools for those who could afford it. In October 1892 it was extended to hospitals with the opening of the Columbus Hospital in New York.

From 1911 Mother Cabrini's health was failing; she was worn out. With St Paul she could speak of having undertaken 'labours more abundant' (2 Cor. 11.23) and like him she had often met opposition from her own people, even to the extent of a law-suit in Italy, but she remained steadfast. There is nothing new in any of her writings, it was not what she said that impressed her sisters but her example. She shared in the whole life of her community down to the dullest jobs. Very early on she had resolved never to ask of her nuns anything that she was not prepared to do herself.

At Eastertide in 1917 she went to her Congregation's house in Chicago but she looked so ill the sisters immediately sent for the doctor. By the summer, after much rest she seemed to be much better, but in November she again became very ill and died suddenly three days before Christmas. In her death the Saint of the Immigrants shared their lot, for she died alone.

PRAYER: *Lord when I am sure what you want, help me to see it through faithfully.*

Frances Xavier Cabrini was canonised in 1946.

Index of Saints